How To Turn Your Kitchen Table Or Spare Bedroom Into A

CASH MACHINE!

by

T.J. Rohleder
"The Blue Jeans Millionaire"

Also by T.J. Rohleder:

The Black Book of Marketing Secrets (Series)
The Ultimate Wealth-Maker
Four Magical Secrets to Building a Fabulous Fortune
The Ruthless Marketing Attack
$60,000.00 in 90 Days
How to Start Your Own Million Dollar Business
Fast Track to Riches
Five Secrets That Will Triple Your Profits
25 Direct Mail Success Secrets That Can Make You Rich
24 Simple and Easy Ways to Get Rich Quick
How to Create a Hot Selling Internet Product in One Day
Secrets of the Blue Jeans Millionaire
Shortcut Secrets to Creating High-Profit Products
Ruthless Copywriting Strategies

FIRST EDITION

ISBN 1-933356-35-9

TABLE OF CONTENTS

INTRODUCTION

Hello there! I'm T.J. Rohleder, co-founder of Mid-American Opportunity Research Enterprises, Incorporated (M.O.R.E., Inc., for short) in Goessel, Kansas. For the last 20 years, I've been making my financial dreams come true in the marketing field, and I'd like to invite you to join me in a new opportunity that I honestly believe can enrich both of us to the tune of *millions* of dollars.

You know, most people who think that they want to be in business really just want the cash flow. It's the *benefits* of being in business that they want, not necessarily the business itself. They want a cash machine that gives them the money that they want, when they want it. So is it possible to actually create such a cash machine, short of counterfeiting money? Is there a perfect moneymaking program out there that offers all the good aspects of a cash machine without being associated with anything negative? **There sure is, and we've got it: CLUB-20 International.** Our parent company, M.O.R.E., Inc., has been studying business opportunities for the last 20 years. We've been recording our findings and separating out the few exceptional business opportunities from all the rest, the ones that are just nothing but a bunch of hype. You see, you've got to have a way to cut through all the clutter in this field because, if you don't, every promoter who comes along is going to sound good to you. They're all enthusiastic about what they're doing, after all. And I'm not talking about the criminals or con-men: I'm talking about the honest, good people, too. That's a requirement for really succeeding in marketing. They love their business opportunities so much, and they're so enthusiastic about them, that if you're not careful, you're going to get sucked into that enthusiasm yourself.

5

But if the opportunity lacks the bare essentials that I'm going to talk about in this book, or if it doesn't have as many of those things as possible... well, let's just say that it's going to be less than optimal for you. **I'm going to cover 65 different points in this book, and any business opportunity you encounter needs to include as many of those 65 points as possible if you expect to succeed. The best opportunities have them all.**

But before we get started, let me tell you a little more about myself and my qualifications. My wife and I started M.O.R.E., Inc. in September 1988, back when we were literally dirt poor. Even then, I was hooked on the idea of making a fortune in marketing. For years, I'd sent away for every plan and program I could get my hands on. I was unhappy with my life as it was, you see. I worked in the oil fields in a town called Great Bend, Kansas, where I grew up. I dropped out of high school so I could go to work, because I hated school. Later, I worked construction, and by the time I was in my early 20s I was working in a factory welding mobile home frames.

And I hated my job *so much*. Every day, I dreaded going to work. I did it for the money — I was making pretty good money for an uneducated blue-collar guy with no skills — and yet every day was a living hell for me. A *literal* hell, too. If you've ever welded for a living, you'll know it's very hot. Plus, it can get up to 110 degrees in Kansas in the summertime, and I worked in a metal building. Even worse, because I was a welder, I had to wear all this heavy clothing. Every day, I dreaded it. I couldn't stand it, and I was miserable — about as miserable as a person can be, without resorting to drugs or alcohol.

But then a friend of mine invited me to this Multi-Level Marketing (MLM) opportunity that he'd just gotten involved in. It made me excited. It was going to make me rich, and we were all going to make millions of dollars! So I got involved in it...

and it never made me a dime. But what it did was expose me to supportive, upbeat people who shared my dream. I went to my first opportunity meeting, and it was full of people who were all pumped up about this opportunity. They drew the circles out and showed me that if I just went out and got five people, who went out and got five more, and then they went and got five, by the time I got down to the 7th level I was going to have half the world's population in my downline — and I was going to have my own island and my own Lear Jet! Man, was I excited! And so. I was an easy sale.

That company went out of business about four months after I got into it, but I was hooked, so I joined one MLM company after another. Within a few years, I'd joined nine of these programs. I never made a dime on any of them — I only lost money — and yet I wasn't as miserable anymore! I was still going to my job as a welder in the factory, and it was still terrible work and I hated it, but I had a dream. And those companies I joined got me reading all these success and motivational books, and I started listening to tapes that I got from the library. I couldn't afford to buy them, but in the Wichita and Newton, Kansas, libraries there were plenty of motivational recordings that you could borrow. So I was subjecting myself to all this good, positive stuff on a daily basis.

And thanks to MLM, I learned that there was another way to make money besides working an hour and getting paid for that hour. I was excited, and I really believed that I could make millions of dollars. I was *that* crazy! And it *was* kind of crazy at the time, because I had no education, no skills, and no knowledge. I wasn't even born with a high IQ or anything: I'm just an average person. To make a long story short, I started buying up all these get-rich-quick opportunities. I got on all the mailing lists. I'd come home at night from a job that I hated, I'd open up my mailbox, and it would just overflow. The mailman could barely get all the offers into my mailbox! All this junk mail would fall out, and I would spend the night reading sales letters about all these different ways I could get rich. I started sending away for every one of these programs I could afford — and even the ones I couldn't.

These opportunities gave me hope, they inspired me, and they got me excited. And ultimately, I met my wife Eileen, and she didn't laugh at me like everybody else did. She was a cashier at a filling station in Newton, and when she saw all these programs I was spending my money on, she didn't laugh at all. She took my dreams seriously, and that was a first for me. Now, she laughed at some of the programs, because I bought some really crazy ones. Eventually, she helped me pick out a few of the features of the better ones and weave them together into our first real product. That's basically what I'll be discussing in this book: how to find the best programs, the ones with the best features, the ones that will truly serve you and help you achieve your dreams. How do you choose the few programs that are really good, versus all of the ones that are just a bunch of hype?

Eileen helped me do that. She's the Queen of Common Sense; my wife has more common sense than anybody I know. She helped me pick out two companies. One was from Chicago, a company called Laser Phase, and another was from a guy in Canada named George Hoskins. **We took those two programs, blended them together, put some of our own ideas into the mix, and started making hundreds of dollars a week right out of the gate.** Then one day, Eileen said something that basically tossed gasoline on the spark of our little business: "You know, I bet you a lot of other people out there would like to do what we're doing." Well, that got me thinking, so I wrote this little booklet called *Dialing for Dollars*. I still hand it out to people who attend my live seminars to show everyone what we started with. *Dialing for Dollars* was based on our mixture of those two business opportunities we were profiting on. We put this little booklet out there, knowing there were other people who were looking for a proven way to make money, and knowing our method was better than anything else we had ever tried. It was actually *working*, and it was the *only* thing that ever worked for us.

Now, our original *Dialing For Dollars* booklet is so small that it's more like a brochure. It's poorly written, filled with typos and grammatical errors. I could barely write at the time! Some say I can barely write now. I'm a little better, but not much. But despite this little booklet's flaws, it outlined a program that really worked and, before long, we had people who were making thousands of dollars a month with it. People who had never made any real money in their lives were actually making money with this program! Some of our distributors were making as much as $20,000, $30,000, $40,000, even $50,000 a month with this little program, because it included some of the features that I'm going to talk about in this book. In fact, one of our distributors, a former lawyer named Jay Peterson out of Provo, Utah, ended up making $5 million a year! That was about three times more money than *we* were making — so it was doing quite well for him!

That's my story in a nutshell. **Over the years, we've built a company out of helping other people make money.** Since those early days, I've fallen in love with the whole Direct-Response Marketing business. I'll be talking a lot more about Direct-Response Marketing throughout this book, because I can't help but talk about that. Only in the last five or six years have my staff and I been committed to figuring out a way to combine MLM with Direct-Response Marketing. **That combination of those two powerful forms of marketing has resulted in our new opportunity, CLUB-20 International.**

I feel that the title of this book is quite apt, because **I really will show you how to turn your kitchen table or a desk in a**

spare bedroom into a cash machine. The idea is that it doesn't take a lot of space. I'm not talking about a business that requires some sort of local office; you don't have to start a company where you have to hire employees. A lot of the headaches and hassles that go along with traditional business are things that most people don't want to get involved with, and I'm guessing you probably don't want to get involved with them either. You want the benefits of running a business, you want the money, you want the freedom, but you don't want the responsibilities of having to worry about a staff. You don't want to have to worry about getting up and opening the doors at 8:00 A.M. to let people in, selling widgets all day, locking up at the end of the day and then preparing to do it all over again, day in and day out. **You want a business that can run itself; the kind of business that's better and more profitable than a traditional job.**

Because let's face it: a lot of people who have local businesses might as well be working for somebody else. They have all the headaches and hassles of a regular job but none of the profits. So I'm talking about businesses here that have big profit potential and yet can be run from a laptop computer that's sitting on your kitchen table. That's all you need. And in many cases, you don't even *need* a table. If you'd like to sit in your easy chair in your living room, that's fine. Want to work from your bedroom? No problem. I do most of my business either here at a desk at the office, in a small amount of space, or on my laptop at home. So things *can* be done in a relatively small amount of space that let you make huge profits. Your business really *can* be like a cash machine.

When I say "cash machine," I get this picture in my head of this old steam locomotive sitting there just pumping out cash — eye-popping, jaw-dropping stacks of cash — and really, that's what it's all about! The idea gets me excited. I don't know anybody who doesn't get excited about big piles of money, especially in this economy!

I really do think this is the greatest business in the world, because you can live your own lifestyle just the way you like it. If you can imagine your ideal, perfect day, you can create that based upon your Direct-Response Marketing business. I'm a living testament that this is possible. Not that long ago, I was sitting right where *you're* sitting. I was reading books and listening to tapes and CDs, saying to myself, "I'd really, really like to make huge sums of money. So how can I do it?"

In this book, we're going to be discussing some the characteristics we look for in any kind of an opportunity we evaluate. Though it's specifically oriented toward our CLUB-20 International distributorship opportunity, it works for anything — whether you're talking about a service, or buying the rights to something that already exists, or creating your own information product. In **Part I,** I'll discuss the 50 most important things to look for when choosing a business opportunity. Here's how it'll work: **I'll present each item and then provide an outline of how CLUB-20 International offers exactly that.** By the end of this half of the book, I'll have told you how CLUB-20 International gives our distributors each and every one of these 50 things. In **Part II,** I'll present the remaining 15 items to look for in any business opportunity; **then I'll provide you with ways to weave all 65 points together to provide the best possible opportunity for your business needs.**

Whatever business you're looking to do, whatever opportunity you're pursuing or considering, I confidently believe that the strategies I'll be discussing here will put you in position to make the most money. **This is the full blueprint that's going to put all the pieces of the puzzle together.** So congratulations for buying this book. I know you'll find it valuable once you read all the secrets I'm offering here. I encourage you to go through it once just to absorb the ideas; then read it again and take some notes, or just jot things in the margins. The second time through, things will be a lot clearer. You'll have a better idea of where I'm coming from and the strategies I teach, as you begin to grasp everything that you need to know in order to make all the money you'll ever need.

PART ONE

The 50 Most Important Things to Look For When Choosing the Perfect Business Opportunity

CHAPTER ONE:

The Acid Test Formula

The first thing I'd like to discuss is what I call the Acid Test Formula. **These are the 12 questions that we always ask ourselves at M.O.R.E., Inc. when we're analyzing any business opportunity.** We've been using this formula since 1988 to expose the very few business opportunities that are a cut above all of the rest. It quickly tells us which ones are worth pursuing and which ones are absolutely a waste of our time. This enables us to go through hundreds of business opportunities every month, and it starts with three simple questions. If we get affirmative answers to all three, we continue to research the opportunity further; if we get negative answers, we drop it like a hot potato.

That's not the end of it, though: we follow through with nine more questions before we're happy. We have to get an affirmative to at least 9 or 10 of these questions before we can determine whether it's an opportunity we want to recommend to our clients. Now, most opportunities can't even make it past the first three; this is what lets us get through so many opportunities so quickly. In fact, most opportunities can't even make it past the <u>FIRST QUESTION</u>: **Are average people already making huge sums of money?**

This is the most important question we ask during our acid test. If the answer is "Yes!," we pursue it. If the answer is "No!," we don't. Simple as that. **We're looking for something that lets average people succeed — that is, people who have no special knowledge, skills, abilities, or training.** If average people are making huge sums of money; then we get excited about the opportunity.

But, the truth is with most opportunities the answer is "No!" The only people that are making decent money are the ones we call the "heavy hitters." These are people who have the brilliance, time, experience, and start-up money to be able to do well right off the bat — which automatically excludes most people. With most opportunities, then, average people are *not* making huge sums of money; they don't stand a chance. So under our Acid Test Formula, neither do most opportunities. You should only look for those opportunities where you know the most average person in the world is already making money; **that's the kind of opportunity that can make money for *you*.** If an opportunity can only be taken advantage of by genius marketers, then that limits the rest of us. Most of us aren't rocket scientists, so we have to look for something within our capabilities.

You can't move on to the second question if an opportunity doesn't meet the first. Why bother? So start by looking at who's making money in this industry. If that person looks like you, there's a potential for you to make a lot of money, too. If I'm looking at any particular opportunity, **I'm going to look for cash-specific testimonials.** I'm going to look for people who have stepped up and said something like, "Hello, my name is T.J. Rohleder from Goessel, Kansas, and I made $15,000 my first month in this business." Are there cash-specific testimonials, and are they believable? If so, it's a good idea to then go to a website like the White Pages (www.whitepages.com) and look them up, to see if you can actually find them and determine if they're being truthful. If you can't find them in the town they're supposed to live in, then that testimonial is probably false.

Even if you can't prove it one way or the other, it's an opportunity you need to bypass — unless you don't mind losing your shirt! **You absolutely *must* look for people who are similar to you.** The more similar they are to you demographically and psychographically — in age, education, income, background, locale, and how they got started — the more likely you are to emulate their success.

My colleague Kent Sayre was recently telling me about an infomercial in which basically, all this famous infomercial marketer did was hire all his business buddies, who are all mega-successful entrepreneurs, to come on and give testimonials as if they were average people. But they *weren't*. So, you have to watch out for that trick. Those people are already experts at making money; they're far from average. You can't do what the guru is doing to make his money; that's a tall order, especially if it looks very difficult or almost magical. You have to make sure you can do what other people are doing to make money in that opportunity, **which is why you need to look for something that's profitable for the average person who's willing to put in the necessary effort.**

Now I'm going to show you how our CLUB-20 International answers the first question of our Acid Test Formula, and how it solves the problems associated with it. It all started about four years ago, when we came across a company out of Panama City, Panama, that was operating a compensation plan similar to the one that we've adopted. Now, we've changed it somewhat, but theirs was similar in this sense: they paid the largest amount of commissions to the smallest groups of distributors. We made $10,000 in our very first week with that opportunity. Since then, we've had some problems with that company's leadership; I'd prefer not to go into the details, but let's just say that one of the leaders of that company was a Ku Klux Klan member. We only found out about that after we were involved for 18 months. I assure you, as soon we discovered that, we were out; we didn't care how profitable the company was, if that was the leadership quality.

But while we were members, we made hundreds of thousands of dollars every month with that opportunity, and it gave us the idea for this compensation plan. That was the thing that got us so excited in the beginning, because in a sense, it was *anti*-MLM. In its traditional form, MLM pays the smallest percentage of the commissions to the largest groups of distributors. **This compensation plan did the opposite.**

Now, are we average people? We are. We really are. Look at me — I'm the most average guy on the planet, and yet I'm President and CEO of a Direct-Response Marketing company that's done over $100 million in sales in our first 20 years. That fact alone would make some people say, "Well, no, T. J., you're *not* average. You've got this huge customer base," and yes, that's true. We tapped into our power base, and we had a large power base to tap into. A great deal of our success had to do with that, I'll admit. However, there were other people who were part of the original MLM company who were extremely average. They didn't have power bases; they were just average people who had never made any significant money in their entire lives, and suddenly they were making $20,000, $30,000, and $40,000 a month or more. It was the first time ever that a lot of these people had made *any* money — and they were making money in spite of certain mistakes that they were making, according to our research.

I think that the important thing to note here is that the foundations of our compensation plan are rooted in that original plan that made us so much money. **CLUB-20 is brand new, but the way we've structured the compensation plan is based on our experiences and results of that original program from a few years back.** Sure, that plan had its problems, but it wasn't all bad, and we wanted to utilize its best features. That's why we've adopted its basic compensation plan, because we knew it was powerful — and we knew it had the potential to make a lot of money fast. When you start with that premise and some of the other things I'll be talking about in this chapter, **what you end up with is the ability to pay a huge commission right upfront** instead of letting our members make just a little bit of money. It's all rooted in the formula based on this first principle: are average people already making huge sums of money? Yes, they sure are.

This is a superbly dynamic, proven compensation plan, and I guarantee you that specialists in Network Marketing will be attracted to it — another thing that should perk your ears up. You see, these Network Marketing guys are super-attracted to fabulous compensation plans. That's the first thing out of their mouths when you talk to them. Often, they don't care about the product or anything else. They'll say, "Have you seen the comp plan?" Well, this comp plan was chosen in part because it's going to attract a large number of Network Marketing guys out there. When they see a hot comp plan they're all over it, and that's what's going to attract somebody's attention. That's another reason we got such a big-time positive answer when we asked that first question.

The SECOND QUESTION is: **Can the opportunity be started for less money than most people can scrape together for something they really want?**

Whenever I consider this question, I always think of my sister, Ann. I love her dearly, and if she ever reads this, I hope she doesn't mind me using her as an example. The fact is, she's been poor all of her life; I hope she changes that eventually. She's always struggled financially, even though she's always been gainfully employed. Yet she always comes up with a way to find money for things she *really* wants. She can always come up with a few hundred dollars for this or a few thousand dollars for that. I realize that most people are like that; they can scrape the money together for something that's exciting enough.

And yet, it's a fact that some things are just too expensive for most people. There's a coffee shop right down the road in Hesston, Kansas, that I like to go to. Well, the folks who own it paid $125,000 to get involved in that opportunity. Before they sold one cup of coffee, they were out $125,000! Look, if the opportunity you're planning to get involved with is too expensive, it's going to be a failure for you. **So look for lower cost opportunities, options that give you the opportunity to succeed from Day One.**

When this subject comes up, my mentor Russ von Hoelscher often tells a story about a guy he was doing some consulting work for. The guy wanted to know what he needed to do to get started. He wanted a product to sell; he already had an office. He'd rented or leased it — probably signed a long-term lease — and he'd hired about 50 employees and had a stack of computers lined up in the office. I mean, he'd put in the infrastructure and was ready to go... and he was looking to Russ to figure out what to sell! *Wrong!* He'd spent way too much money on infrastructure and not enough time and energy figuring out what he was going to sell *first*.

If it takes a lot of money to get started, then avoid that business. It's too complicated. If you have to invest in a lot of infrastructure, forget it. And if you have no idea what you're going to sell, you're shooting yourself in the foot. You need to be able to get started for as little as possible and get money coming in right away.

Again, though, you'd be surprised what kind of money people will find when they really want something. Have you ever seen that show COPS? It's amazing. They'll go into this guy's house, and it's just falling apart... but as they're slapping the cuffs on him, he's saying, "Hey, how do you like my new 65-inch TV?" **People find the money for the things they want!** So if you're creating an opportunity, you don't want to come up with a plan that's way out of most people's leagues, but you do want to get paid for what it's worth. If they want it, they're going to find the money for it.

It's crucial to consider this in pricing an opportunity. It's true that if you price something too high, then you may price it right out of an ordinary person's reach; however, you do have to remember that **people will spend money on things they want, as long as that price is reasonable, and they can see the value in it.** After all, if everybody always bought the cheapest thing, then we'd all be driving really cheap cars, wouldn't we? And yet there are a lot of cars that cost a *lot* more than your base car. You can get a really cheap car for around $10,000 if you hunt for one — a really cheap *new* car. And yet, you can also spend $50,000 on a luxury model, or even more.

Therefore, even if your opportunity costs a few thousand dollars, if people really can see the value in it, if they see that it has great potential, then they can scrape up that price. **So it's all about building value and making people see that value.** Most people will find the money for something if you can compare it to a weekend vacation in Las Vegas or what it would cost to buy a big screen TV.

So when you're researching an opportunity, **you need to look for one where the target market is irrationally passionate, has money to spend, and is reachable through Direct-Marketing.** Now, CLUB-20 International has all those three things, and we've priced this perfectly, so that people can come up with the cash to get in on this opportunity. Plus, it's backed by a world-class sales and marketing machine — and I believe those two things are going to make this opportunity very, very successful.

With CLUB-20 International, you're getting an opportunity to make huge amounts of money, and it only costs about as much to get started as you'd spend to go away for a long weekend. Wouldn't you trade a weekend vacation for the potential to make thousands of dollars a month? That's something people can easily see the value of. It has to be cheap enough to get started that people can see making that payment. And that means, in most cases, that you want to stay in that sweet spot (as we call it) where people are comfortable finding the money to spend when you compare it to something they would do, like going away for a weekend. **With CLUB-20 International, you really** *can* **start for about the cost of a four-day vacation in Vegas — so it's reasonably priced.**

Here's the THIRD QUESTION in our Acid Test Formula: **Is it possible to make thousands of dollars right away?**

For most opportunities, the answer is a resounding, "No!" You can avoid them. **A good opportunity has to be structured in such a way that it allows you to profit immediately.** In most MLM companies, you have to build a huge downline before you ever make any real money. Well, that takes time. This time-lag isn't unusual with most businesses, in fact; a lot of companies have to build a large customer base before they can make any money. The U.S. Department of Commerce estimates that it takes an average of two to five years before you can make your first profit. Well, if you're involved in a business like that, forget it — because you need money *now*. **So look for an opportunity where there's a history of average people who have made a lot of money quickly.**

The best way to do that is to look for products within that opportunity that offer high profit margins. Most businesses sell things that offer narrow, even razor-thin profit margins; think about Wal-Mart-type products. Now, Wal-Mart has expensive items, like TVs and DVD players and other electronics, but go down the average aisle at Wal-Mart and you're seeing inexpensive items. That's kind of Wal-Mart's

22

whole point. If you're buying a 99-cent stick of deodorant, or some toothpaste, or some toilet paper, there's not very much profit in that, even if Wal-Mart gets to keep all the money. So when you're looking at opportunities, don't fall for the nickel-and-dime ones. If you sell a two-dollar item and you get to keep all of it, you make two bucks. Wow! Well, if you sell a $1,000 item and get to keep half of it, you make $500. If you want to be able to put yourself in a position to make thousands of dollars, the way to do that is *not* by selling cheap stuff where you get to keep a little bit of money every time you make a sale. **You want high-ticket items, because that's where the money is.** You want to sell things that have maximum value so that you can keep the most money on every transaction.

What sounds better? "Here's an opportunity that can help you make ends meet…" Or, "Here's an opportunity that can put thousands of dollars in your pocket next month... next week... right now!" You're going to see that over and over again, because it's the kind of copywriting that stimulates people's greed glands and gets their attention. But you definitely want to go back and be realistic about it. Is it possible to make a lot of money right away? Because if it isn't, if the money doesn't start flowing, people lose their interest. They lose their motivation, and they're gone. **If an opportunity doesn't let you put some money in your pocket pretty quickly, run away!**

One of the interesting things about CLUB-20 is that it functions on two different fronts. Making thousands of dollars right away is exciting, because you can get into it inexpensively and start profiting immediately. That's very good, because seeing is believing. You think, "Hey, this thing is for real!" And then you can start to crank up your efforts and make even more money. Plus, there's the recruiting aspect. When you're going to someone else and saying, "Hey, get in on this opportunity," and you can prove it's profitable, *that's* when the sales machine really kicks in. Being able to say, "Hey, I made thousands of dollars right away…" is a lot more compelling than having to work like a dog for two to five years before you can even begin to turn a profit. So many people live in what I like to call a "microwave mentality," in that if they can't start to see results in the time it takes to pop popcorn, then they'll want to throw in the towel. **So making thousands of dollars right away is crucial to your average opportunity seeker,** if only because it gets people off to a good start. Momentum is so powerful!

And is it possible to make thousands of dollars right way with CLUB-20 International? Absolutely! **This opportunity pays you $1,000** *on every sale.* A thousand dollars, right away. That beats most opportunities all hollow: you've got to sell a lot of $10 widgets to make thousands of dollars. But if you get paid $1,000 on each transaction — like you do with CLUB-20 — well, it doesn't take too much, does it? Just one of those every day and most people are making more money than they've ever dreamed of making. In fact, at that rate, most people make more money in that first month than some people make in a year! Even if you average just one transaction a day, you'll be making $30,000 a month. All it takes is a little math to realize that's $360,000 a year — which is a darn good income in anyone's book. But it gets better! **With CLUB-20, we pay $1,000 to you for every sale we make for you** *and* **$1,000 for every sale we make for the people we place on your team.** So you have the ability to make thousands of dollars right away, and our automated system does the selling for you — which makes it even easier!

So far, we've answered the first three questions in our Acid Test. Those three questions are the most crucial when analyzing any opportunity. If the opportunity won't let you do all three of those things, then just stay away from it. **You've got to be able to make money fast, you've got to be able to get started cheaply; and average people have to already be making good**

money. If the answer is "Yes!" to all three of those questions, you move on to the rest. Those first three are foundational; and as we've demonstrated, **CLUB-20 International is a winner all three ways.**

The <u>FOURTH</u> <u>QUESTION</u> in our twelve-point Acid Test Formula is: **Can everything be done from the comfort, privacy, and security of your own home?**

Again, with a lot of opportunities the answer is "No!" You either have to have a retail location, or you have to be on the road constantly. Who wants that? You should look for opportunities that let you stay home and make money from the comfort, privacy, and security of your own home. **For it to be the perfect opportunity, it has to give you the freedom to be able to do that.**

As I mentioned in the introduction, you've got to be able to get started in a small amount of space. Now, even if a retail space isn't required, a lot of businesses that you can, say, run in the mall require a kiosk or a traveling cart. Once we looked at a coffee opportunity where you had a truck that you drove around to businesses. And although the opportunity was great, there was a big vehicle involved, and you had to buy the vehicle. That gets expensive! **So if you can't do it from the comfort and privacy of your own home, costs start to add up.** There are other factors involved, of course, and you just don't want to get involved with them. Or at least, we at M.O.R.E., Inc. don't want to, and I think the majority of our customers feel the same way. Now, of course, some people don't, and there are certainly people who are successful in those kinds of businesses. But we believe the average person should stay away from them.

My buddy Chris Hollinger likes CLUB-20 International simply because he has this romantic notion of being able to work out of a cabin in Montana. Of course, his wife would never go for it, but still, he'd love to do that! And that brings up another good point you should ask yourself, a kind of sub-question when examining a new opportunity: **what's going to be required of you, and when, how and *where* can you concentrate on this business opportunity?** Is the company going to be pushing you to go out and talk to people, or call them on the phone to sell the opportunity? What exactly is the process? Just by having this question in front of you and asking, "Is this something that I can do from home... legitimately?" you're going to get rid of a lot of contenders.

And there's what I think is the larger issue you need to consider: **can this business opportunity fit into your lifestyle?** This is where you need to start when considering the question. What *is* your lifestyle? I'm a big proponent of lifestyle design and figuring out exactly how you can live your life on your own terms, according to your own rules. Well, this is a business opportunity that can fit those requirements. **It's flexible; it can fit into your predetermined lifestyle.** That's very unlike the way most people think of a job, irrespective of who you are or your lifestyle. They expect to adjust to the job — this is the job, these are the hours to work, and this is how much you're going to get paid every hour. You might have to work with people you don't like. You might have to do a thankless job. Even if you take on a business opportunity and become your own boss, you may be forced to travel; many such opportunities require you to go to trade shows or flea markets, or be on the road constantly. Or they force you to have a retail location where you're away from home, and you're always in the store or in the office somewhere. Not every opportunity can be done from home. CLUB-20 offers the difference between you conforming, for example, to a franchise with multiple restrictions — or choosing this perfect business that fits your dream lifestyle. That can make all the difference in the world to your happiness.

One of the big reasons CLUB-20 makes life so easy for the entrepreneur is that we have an automated system where we do all the work for you. That frees up your time for what *you* want to do. You don't have to have a big box of merchandise to ship out every day. You don't have to have storage space. You don't have to have anything, really, at home. Our system does everything for you. Our main product is a three-day event called the "Wealth Explosion Seminar," and obviously, you can't ship a seminar. People attend it, so you're selling a product that doesn't need to be delivered.

We take care of all the confirmations, all the fulfillment. We take care of your clients for you. And our automated system actually helps make the sales for you, so there's *nothing* needed on your end, except your investment. You can literally work the business wherever you are — and the business can continue to work for you without your direct input, whether you're on vacation in Hawaii, at your home in Florida or Minnesota, or halfway around the world enjoying a quiet beach somewhere. **You can be doing anything anywhere, because our automated system does most of the work for you.** Club 20 International requires very little hands-on involvement and very little space.

Here's the FIFTH POINT that we look for when applying our Acid Test Formula: **Can someone make huge sums of money in their spare time?**

If the money you're earning has little or nothing to do with the amount of time that you put into the enterprise, then the answer is "Yes!" If it has more to do with that, then the answer is "No!" A lot of opportunities simply force you to put in tremendously long hours. Now, if it's a labor of love, if it's something that gives you great joy and pleasure, then that's one thing. But if it's taking you away from other things that are important to you, that's another. **So we look for opportunities**

where the money you make has nothing to do with the hours you actually spend working. That way, you're getting paid on other things besides your time: you're getting paid on other people's efforts, on the products and services being sold. Therefore, you can make tremendous amounts of money even if you're working part-time, and you can kick back and enjoy life.

When you think about it, unless you're making millions of dollars, **why should you put up with the headaches and hassles of a regular job?** Why would you want to get into a business that forced you to work long hours? I think about some of the local businesses in my area — coffee shops, restaurants, and things like that — where the owners are there all the time, and they're constantly heavily involved. They're the first ones there in the morning and the last ones to leave; they spend all their lives there, basically. They might as well be working for somebody else. That way, they'd be able to go home in the evening and not have to worry about the business. But they get all the headaches and hassles — *and* they're not making very much money in return.

So you need to be able to make a lot of money in your spare time. I wrote earlier about a lifestyle business; that is, you want your dream lifestyle to fit around your business, and you want your business to give you the freedom to be able to enjoy that lifestyle. Otherwise, it's not worth it! There's a big difference between those who get up, go to a job, and work for an hourly wage or a salary and someone like me and most of my colleagues. We have promotional-based incomes; that is, our incomes are based on promotions we run or money machines that we build and maintain to keep turning out those profits. There's a big difference when it comes down to those lifestyle issues.

So can you really set something up once and have it pay you again and again? **Absolutely — and you must! Continuity is very important.** You can construct your business to do that, so that you can allocate your time the way you want it, period. *You* determine how you want to live your life, because you have the mechanisms and income streams in place that allow you to live the life that you want.

You've only got so many hours in the day when you're awake and active, and most of us already have that time allocated pretty tightly. You've already got an active, full life, given that you're juggling family, friends, and possibly your career. Or maybe you're retired; well, you've got hobbies and such, right? You've got things to do and people to meet. So where are the hours you'll need to put into a demanding business opportunity going to come from? **That's why it's so crucial to make huge sums of money in your spare time.** Frankly, the average person just isn't going to be able to put in hours upon hours.

With CLUB-20 International, you're getting paid on the sale of the products sold by our automated system. As I've mentioned, our flagship product is a three-day, wealth-making event called the Wealth Explosion Seminar. The automated system sells that for you. Plus, you're getting paid whenever the people who purchase that program from you also decide to become distributors. We place them right into your team — and then you get a generous commission for every sale they make. **That allows you to get paid for things other than the time, work, and effort that you put into the opportunity.**

Now, imagine a system in place where you could have a team of people who are all out there using our automated system, and you're getting paid $1,000 every time we help *them* make a sale. So let's say you had 10 people on your team, and those 10 people each went out and made just one sale a month using our automated system. Those 10 people would each be making $1,000 a month, because they're making one sale, and they get paid $1,000 on that automated sale. But because they're on your team, *you* get a check for $10,000, just because those 10 people each made one sale. **That's 10 sales, total, for your team — and a $10,000 bonus check just showing up at your door for all the work that we did to help *them* make one sale each per month. Ten thousand dollars!** That's automated cash. *That's* the kind of thing we're talking about here: huge amounts of money in your spare time.

And how much spare time did that require of you, for those 10 people to use our automated system? Nothing. Zero. Zilch. **You didn't do anything, because *we* were helping them make sales, but because they're in your team, you got paid $1,000 for each sale that we helped them make. Beyond that, you also get paid $1,000 for each automated sale that we make for *you*.** If you're using our automated system and making just one sale a month, you'd be getting $1,000 a month automatically. If you were making 10 sales a month, you'd get $10,000 automatically. And again, our automated system means that you spend as little time as possible actually working the business.

Now, there's *one* thing you do have to do. Our automated system revolves around giving away my free book, *$60,000 In 90 Days*. To accomplish that, you can run classified ads; you can mail postcards; you can do free advertising — you can do anything you want to give away my free book. **We only ask for $5 shipping and handling to help prove the prospects are serious and to weed out the folks who'll take anything if it's free.** Incidentally, that's much less money than it costs to print it up; this is no cheap little booklet, this is a full-fledged, softcover book, beautifully printed, full-color cover and all. The book costs us *considerably* more than $5 to print — and certainly, we have to pay the shipping anyway.

Again, the S&H fee is just to prove they're serious. **But we'll ship the book out for that $5 and take care of everything else.** We do all the follow-up. We talk to them on the phone; we answer their questions; we invite them to tele-seminars — we do everything we can to show them the value of purchasing the flagship product. And when they do purchase, we automatically send you a $1,000 commission just for that sale. That happens over and over again. **All you have to do is advertise to give away the book.** And, again, we call this an automated system for a reason — because we can even do that one step for you! Right now isn't the time to talk about that, so we'll get to it later. But rest assured, we do have systems in place so that you don't even have to do the advertising. That's what allows you to work in your spare time. Actually, instead of saying "spare time," maybe I should say "no time!" You can certainly arrange it that way.

Question <u>NUMBER SIX</u> that you should ask about any opportunity is: **Is it possible to make millions of dollars?**

Some people don't want to make millions of dollars. But, again, **we're looking for an opportunity where it's possible to make tremendous amounts of money.** Remember the coffee shop in Hesston? The owners are great people. They've got a wonderful little coffee house next to the freeway. But the freeway in Kansas is a little different than the freeway in California or Chicago or Philadelphia. I mean, let's face it: they are never going to make millions of dollars — and they probably don't want to.

Not everybody needs to make millions, either. In fact, some people who think they want to make millions would be happy with just hundreds of thousands of dollars — they just don't know it yet. There's a certain level of money that gives a person what they want and need, and after that, it really doesn't provide any added benefit. I know that's easy for me to say, right? Nothing used to upset me more than listening to or reading about rich celebrities saying, "Oh, money just isn't that important to me." Of *course* money is important to them, or they

31

wouldn't keep it! And I'd think, "Well, hey — give it to me if it's not that important to you!"

But we like opportunities that have the *potential* to make that kind of money. Those are what we call the "perfect" business opportunities. Not every opportunity is capable of it, and it depends on a lot of different factors. Again, it's important to note that this question states, "Is it *possible* to make millions of dollars?" It doesn't say, "Are you going to make millions of dollars within your first 30 days?" There's the *potential* for big profits. If we decide it's possible to make millions of dollars with an opportunity, then we'll take a closer look at it. Now as I've mentioned, not everybody wants or needs to make millions of dollars. Maybe you'd be happy with $10,000 a month. Maybe you'd be happy with $50,000 or $100,000 a month. Whatever your goal, we want an opportunity that has the potential to make profits. So in a sense, "millions of dollars" is just a general term for "big profit potential." **If it doesn't have the potential to make huge amounts of money, we stay away from it.** Now, it might take a few months to build up to that level, or it may take a few years, but we want an opportunity that has big profit potential, even if we start out making a lesser amount. We're not looking for immediate overnight riches here. **We're looking for something that's steady and reliable and has big time profits.**

And, it has to be red-hot, believable, and compelling. You want an offer that's going to get people's attention. It's got to grab them and say, **"Look, this is what's possible! And not only is it possible, but it's realistic that someone average, even you, could go out there and make this kind of money!"** If you don't have that red-hot offer, if there's something lacking in your sales material or in your pitch or in that particular offer and it doesn't grab people's attention, then it's going to be somewhat lackluster — and so are the potential profits. So when you're looking for that big profit potential, also ask yourself, "Is it realistic, and does it grab people's attention?" If the answer is "Yes!" then keep moving forward in the decision process.

Also, as with any business opportunity, you need to ask yourself, "What is the downside, and what is the upside?" **What you're looking to do is hedge the downside in relationship to the upside.** Think about it like this: let's say you're playing roulette in a casino. You have $5,000 in chips, and you're ready to do some outrageous gambling — and you've got it all on either black or red. Given the green 0 and 00, that's less than a 50-50 proposition that you could lose $5,000, or you could gain $5,000. I don't like those odds, and that's why I'm not a casino gambler.

With CLUB-20 International, you change the odds drastically in your favor. The downside odds are slim — but the upside odds are incredibly large! **That's what's so exciting about CLUB-20: the upside is so huge, and you *do* have the potential to make millions and millions of dollars.** So this is a no-brainer.

Just to give you an example of what's possible: with our compensation plan, if you have 10 distributors on your team who average 10 sales each per month, that's $100,000 a month for you. **That's over a million a year. There's no promise or guarantee that you'll make millions of dollars, but the *potential* is there.** Like any ideal business opportunity, it's set up to give the right kind of people the ability to make millions if they really want to. Or maybe you're happy with $50,000 or $60,000 extra a year; well, you've got the ability to make that, too, since a system that has the ability to make millions also has the ability to make tens of thousands. **So whatever your comfort level, whatever the lifestyle you choose — this business can do it for you.** If you're comfortable with just a few thousand dollars a month, well, how easy does that seem? With our system, you could make an extra $3,000 a month just by letting our automated system make you three sales a month. If you wanted to have a team of people, and you said, "I need at least $10,000 a month to be happy," well, all you need is to get a few other people on your team, with each of you making one every month. That's it. It's easy to do the math. You make $1,000 on every sale we make for you, *and* you make $1,000 for every sale we make for the people we get to join your team. The math is real simple; it's just $1,000 each, times "x" number of sales. You can do the math in your head and easily do it on paper.

Of course, there are other ways to make money, too, besides that $1,000... but I won't complicate the issue by going into all that right now. Suffice it to say, besides our flagship product we have other products that we're selling, and **there are other ways for you to make automatic money.** But for now, we're going to keep it simple just by letting you know that there are other opportunities built in beyond that $1,000 commission.

Here's the <u>SEVENTH</u> <u>QUESTION</u> in our 12-question Acid Test Formula: **Can you make huge sums of money with no personal selling?**

Now, I'm a salesman, and I'm proud of it. I wasn't always proud to be a salesman, but I'm proud of it now, and the older I get, the *more* I'm proud of it. And yet, I have to admit that **personal selling is a tough way to make money.** You have to face rejection all day long. You've got to make all your sales face-to-face. That's a young person's game. I don't want to play that anymore; it's limiting. **Any opportunity that forces you to sell face-to-face every single day is *not* a good opportunity.** So what you're looking for is an opportunity where other systems and other people are doing the selling for you, so you don't have to be dependent on your own personal efforts every day. **When we find opportunities that allow you to make money without direct personal selling, we know then that those are the perfect opportunities.**

What we're looking for here, then, is automated

systems. Obviously, no money is made unless something gets sold, and the only way something gets sold is if somebody or something sells it. Now, you've got salespeople who go door-to-door and make sales. You've got stores that make sales, that have employees and shelves, and run ads and do things to get you into the store. That option's not available for most individuals. With most opportunities the average person is going to get into, there's a lot of personal selling involved.

So we ask ourselves, does the opportunity have some kind of automated system in place that eliminates the need for personal selling? Do they use Direct-Response? Do they give you a website? Do they set things up so you don't have to spend your time talking to people on the telephone? **If they do all that, you can just sit back and let the automated system do all the work for you.** That's the kind of thing I'm talking about here.

What I like about Direct-Response Marketing and Online Marketing is that both give you the ability to have little personal salesmen out there on the Internet or out there in the mail, sitting in someone's desk, next to their toilet, or wherever they're doing their reading. A good sales letter is a personal selling instrument that can go out and work for you 24/7, in thousands of individual copies, whereas personal selling is pretty much one-on-one. **There's a big difference between that and Direct-Response Marketing.** The latter can be personalized. It can be targeted and focused, almost like it's talking to a single person. Obviously, it doesn't have the same essential human nature to it, but these are still selling materials and instruments that can go out there and work for you.

A big reason personal selling is bad news for most people is that they don't like rejection, and that's impossible to avoid in face-to-face situations. Besides, personal selling isn't scalable. There are only a certain number of hours in a day, and if you're doing personal selling, there are only so many people you can call or see per day. Even if you're the greatest salesman on the planet, your income is limited by the hours you work. You've got to sleep; you've got to take breaks; you've got to eat. So if you're doing personal selling, it's not scalable, and you can't roll it out big. **That's why having a system that's *not* built around doing personal selling is the very best option.** All modesty aside, our sales material is some of the best in the business opportunity field. **By using the materials and system we've devised for CLUB-20 International, you don't have to go through any troublesome learning curve of facing rejection and learning how to overcome objections, because it's all done for you.**

With CLUB-20 International, **we provide the sales force.** We call them "client service representatives" because it sounds better — but they're salespeople, okay? Some people, especially some of our new clients, would be offended if we officially called them "salespeople," because nobody wants to be sold anything. **People like to *buy* things, but nobody wants to be *sold* anything.** Therefore, it's more politically correct to call them client service representatives, but the truth is, they're very good salespeople. We're proud of them. Our sales manager, Drew Hansen, has put a great department together — and we're still building it. We have six full-time people now, but we have room to comfortably seat 12. And beyond that, we've got a lot of room upstairs that's not being used.

Hey, our goal is to build this thing. **Our client service representatives sell to the leads that you and the distributors on your team generate.** It's a win-win-win situation! Our salespeople win. Each time they make a sale for you, they make a commission for themselves. They're out to feed their families and they're out to make money, so they're compensated for every sale that they make for you. You win because you get $1,000 for every sale they make for you *and* $1,000 for every sale your distributors make for you. And we win, as a company, because we benefit. We're not making $1,000 off that initial sale, but we do quite well for ourselves.

I'll let you know this right up-front: **all the leads we generate on the behalf of our distributors go into the same lead group as our own leads, so our salespeople can't tell the difference between one of yours and one of ours.** We do that very deliberately, so that for the sales reps, a sale is a sale is a sale. They're out to make as many as they possibly can, period. They get no extra advantage for making a sale for us rather than you; they don't know the difference. The management knows where those leads are all tracked to, of course, but the individual sales rep doesn't. So when they're on the phone with one of your leads, they're going full force just as much as they would with any other lead.

Every week, as leads come in for our various offers — as people request information — those prospects get divided up among all the sales reps so that they can call them back, answer any questions they have, help them work through the order process, and take their orders and get them started. Again, all the leads we get are going to be mixed in with all of the leads that *you* get using our system, so the sales reps won't know whether they're calling somebody who came in through mailings we're doing, or through something you did. **All the leads are treated the same.**

So when we say you can make huge sums of money with no personal selling, we mean it. **You literally don't have to do** *any* **personal selling.** You can use our automated system to bring in the leads — people who want the free book — and when they respond to that offer, it tells them they're also going to receive a special report about a very special opportunity we have for them. So they know they're not just getting a free book. When they request that book, they go into our system. Not only do we have sales reps who call them to answer their questions, we also mail them multiple invitations to join us, as well as invitations to call and talk to one of our sales reps. We invite them to our tele-seminars. Periodically, we'll have conference calls where we answer their questions or show them how they can get started. And we haven't even talked about one of the free gifts we give people: **we make people distributors for free so that we can actually speak to them from a position of authority.**

You can become a distributor for CLUB-20 for only $97 a year, with the first year free. That doesn't give you any of the products, and there's a qualification process that new distributors have to go through. **We give away that position when people request information from us.** We're glad to do so, so that we can get them started. Now, the qualification process limits your ability to make money fast; you have to give up your first four sales. **You can make money faster by purchasing the seminar and bypassing the qualification process, so we advise people to go ahead and do that.**

But everybody gets that entry-level distributor position, so we can go to them and say, "Hey, you're already a distributor, so you should get started right now! And by the way, if you get started now and you make sales, you have to give up your first four sales." That's instantly $4,000 in commissions you're going to lose by being an entry-level distributor, and not only that, you have to give up the commissions on all the sales *those* people make. So if those four people each went out and made just one sale, that would be $8,000 you were giving up as an entry-level distributor. If each of those people made two sales, you'd be giving up $12,000 in commissions. **So there's a lot of money to be lost by going through the qualification process.** Again, if you purchase your own seminar ticket, you can bypass that and start making those commissions from Day One.

It all starts with my book, *$60,000 In 90 Days*. **It's a book**

that sells on Amazon.com for $19.95 — or people can get it
**absolutely free, with a $5 shipping and handling charge that
doesn't even cover the cost of printing.** The book costs us just
under $7 to print, because it's 427 pages. It's not cheap. But
we're giving it away for free. We're asking for a $5 shipping and
handling fee simply so people will prove that they're serious.

When they get the book, we offer them — absolutely free
— an additional gift that's worth almost $100 — $97, to be
exact. It's that free entry-level position. **So they get the free
book,** *and* **they become a distributor.** The beauty of that is that,
now, those people will pay more attention to us. People are so
inundated today with all kinds of offers in all kinds of media;
their heads are just crammed full of information. Don't you feel
that way sometimes? You've got information overload — it's the
disease of the 21st Century! We just have too much stuff going
on. We've got too many things we're trying to keep track of. We
get just too much, too much, too much! So what you've got to
do, as a marketer, is figure out a way to separate yourself from
everybody else, to try to get people's attention and interest, to
get them involved a little. That's tough to do.

So we're going out with our best foot forward. I mean —
absolutely free! That's a *great* offer. You can either go to
Amazon.com and get the book for $19.95 plus shipping and
handling, or you can get it from us for only the $5 shipping and
handling fee. **And it's a book that's designed to get people's
attention.** It's so big that it's got that "thud" factor if you toss it
on a table. We did it that way on purpose to impress people.
Now, we know that very few people will read it cover-to-cover
— most people will skim it, at best. But at least it makes a good
first impression. **And the book comes with our 32-page
invitation that explains everything to them.** It lays out the
option of becoming an entry-level distributor and going through
the qualification process, or upgrading immediately. It actually

serves us better as a company if they go through the qualification, but still get involved in the marketing system, because we keep those first commissions. But we encourage them to upgrade anyway, because we all make more money whenever they get involved at a higher level. People who are just distributors but never buy the product they sell are never going to be that good as distributors. So we want people to go ahead and get involved, to purchase our seminar. **This makes you, the members, more money; it makes us more money; and, quite frankly, it gives us a better-quality distributor.**

Question <u>NUMBER</u> <u>EIGHT</u> in the Acid Test: **Is there help, support, and guidance available from experts with a *proven* track record for making *millions* of dollars?**

Look, there are a lot of good people out there who want to help you make money. And there are a lot of business experts who have never been in business for themselves — but, damn, they can sure tell you how to run yours! **What you want to do is look for people with a track record of excellent past performance, people who make the bulk of their income by helping *you* make money.**

With a lot of opportunities, you're left to figure everything out on your own. **What we look for is a system where there's a lot of help, support, and guidance available.** In general, when you're evaluating opportunities, you want to examine the infrastructure of the company. You want to look for the support. Are there people available to help you? It's sort of like getting a franchise. When you buy a franchise, you get lots of help — often a cookie cutter system — but it's still help that's effective in the long run. What we're after is something like that, but without some of the headaches that go along with a franchise, and there are many. So do you have help, support, and guidance from someone who's doing, or has already accomplished, what you're trying to accomplish? **If a system like that is already in**

place, you have a much better chance of success.

Earlier, I discussed using Direct-Response Marketing and Online Marketing and advertising to go out there and get past the personal selling angles. Well, imagine an opportunity that provides you with the best, most top-notch copywriting available, and sales materials that help convince people that it's something they want to get involved in. If you have a company or an organization that's going to provide you that — and it's proven, and they've made millions of dollars with it — it's pretty much a no-brainer to say, "Okay, I don't know much about copywriting, but T.J. does. **And I can use the same sales letter that's already making sales... I can use the same ad that's already generating leads. Or I can have it all done for me!**" So is it there, or isn't it? If that support and guidance isn't there, the question pretty much answers itself.

One of the great things about CLUB-20 is that it's like marketing with training wheels. You're still riding a bike, but you've got some training wheels on, and even as you're learning, as you're gaining more confidence, you can still have money coming in. And once you start to get the hang of it and you see that money coming in, you say, "Hey, you know what? I might want to learn a little more marketing, because I want to make even more money!" And that's when you can take the training wheels off and become a good, solid marketer in your own right.

Here's a secret I'd like to share that I've found very, very powerful: **stick with one person and one model.** There's something out there that I like to call "guru confusion," and it's caused by the fact that different experts are going to be telling you different things. If you study a number of business opportunities from different people, that can sometimes leave you more confused than when you started. **So, instead of going through all sorts of different business opportunities, stick with one and incorporate it into your moneymaking plan.** Of

41

course, I'd like to encourage you to pick mine! I've got a total blueprint for you.

With CLUB-20 International, our success is tied into *your* **success.** Sure, we're out there generating our own leads, making our own sales, but your leads are stacked in with ours. You're helping us, and we have a vested interest in helping you. The fact that we've got a 20-year business model here with an infrastructure to support you as a distributor and client is important. A lot of companies might offer an email address — and maybe you hope someone gets back to you when you write — but we've had the same phone number for the last 19 years, except that they changed our area code 10 or 15 years ago. Our address is the same: we're in the old hospital building here in Goessel, Kansas. It's easy to find us. You might have to look the town up on a map and drive here, but we're here. **We're a real company with real people.** We've got a staff of about 20 who are here to serve you as clients, affiliates, and distributors, and we put all that infrastructure to work on your behalf. That's what separates us from a lot of other companies, where maybe you've got an email address, and you wait three or four days to get a reply back. I can tell you that we usually respond to email very fast, and if you call in and need to talk to one of our client service representatives, they're usually available. Or you can send a fax; we've got four or five fax machines in the office. The point is **we're here to help and support all our members and distributors, and that's something that separates us from most other companies out there** who are trying to do it on a shoestring.

When it comes to us helping you, **we spend our money to help** *you* **make money.** As of this writing, we're getting ready for the premiere of our Wealth Explosion Seminar. On that promotion alone, we've got at least 30 different follow-up mailings scheduled just to make that sale.

While we want "yes" answers to all our Acid Test Formula questions, the <u>NINTH ONE</u> is really valuable: **Is it a long-term opportunity?**

We're only looking for things that are going to be long-term. So many opportunities out there are faddish; they're hot one day and cold the next. If you're one of the first people involved in them, you might be able to make a lot of money, sure. But ultimately, the person who's left holding the bag at the end... well, you don't want to be that person. **We're looking for long-term business opportunities that involve growing trends and big markets.**

Some fad opportunities can make you a little money and, sometimes, even a lot of money. Recently there was a fad for something called "The Snuggie" that looks like a blanket with sleeves, and you wear it. They've got commercials, and FOX News even did a parody commercial of it. It was a huge success. Those kinds of things can make millions of dollars in a really fast time! I don't want to tell you to avoid that, because if you have an opportunity that can make you millions like that, you *do* want to jump on it. But in general, you want to look at opportunities that have long-term potential because for every Snuggie or ShamWow out there, there are a bunch of other products that ultimately flop. You get involved with them, you sink a lot of money into advertising, nothing comes of it, and that fad is gone. **So you want to stick with long-term opportunities that have the potential to make you profits, not only now but well into the future.** Is it going to be good for someone — and for you — a year from now? Two years from now? What about on down the road?

It's crucial to know whether something is a long-term opportunity or not. And here's the reason why: it comes down to something called **"opportunity costs."** What this means is that when you're doing one thing, you're *not* doing something else.

That is, if you spend an hour watching TV, you're not out exercising. So the opportunity cost of you watching an hour of TV is that you're not in the gym on the treadmill. Similarly, a faddish opportunity is going to cost you, because it's going to keep you from getting involved in something that's consistently profitable. **In other words, if your opportunity doesn't have an explosion in sales and profits, and it's not long-term, then what you cost yourself is a chance to join another, longer-term opportunity.** Given that your time is limited, you want to think long-term, to find something that can grow with you.

CLUB-20 International is a long-term opportunity, because we're targeting two primary markets. One is small business owners, people who have 50 employees or less. We sell products, services, and opportunities that are specifically designed to help those folks make more money by becoming better marketers, specifically by learning Direct-Response Marketing and Information Marketing. These are both things we specialize in, and they both can be used by small business people to dramatically improve their profits and sales. Most don't understand Direct-Response Marketing, so they're not using it. If they did, it would make a significant impact on their businesses. It's getting harder to compete now days, so most small business people are struggling at one level or another. Even those who aren't always want to make more money, so what we've got to teach is music to their ears. It gives them a competitive advantage their competitors don't have. That always gets their attention, so in that market, our product will always be in vogue.

The second market we serve is made up of people who want to go into business for themselves. There's an increasing number of these people, especially with the Baby Boomer generation retiring. That's the group of people who were born from 1946 to 1964, give or take a few years, depending on who you ask. There are 73 million of us out there — and we ain't getting any younger, are we?

And there's a funny thing that happens when somebody gets around 50 years old: I've seen it over and over again within my own family. It seems that's a magical time for them, because all of a sudden, even if they were never serious before, they start thinking about things they didn't before. Like, "Oh my God, I'd better get on the ball here!" The window of opportunity is closing, so they start to see that there's a greater sense of urgency. The Baby Boomers are going to find out two things: first of all, retirement isn't everything they thought it was. I watched my Dad go through that with his retirement, and I watched my step-dad do the same. They dreamed of being retired, and then they *got* retired — and it wasn't good for either man. I don't know exactly how to explain that to you, but let's just say that it wasn't a good experience. It wasn't positive.

You know, my Dad had an active career, and he was kind of a big fish in a very small pond. The phone was constantly ringing. He had all kinds of people wanting to take him out to lunch all the time because they wanted something from him, and he had all these co-workers he loved to work with. And then, all of a sudden, he retired… and their lives kept on going just like before. He was the one who "got out of the stream," so to speak. All of a sudden the phone wasn't ringing anymore, and nobody was asking him to go to lunch or do anything else.

And not only is retired life boring, the second thing the Boomers are going to find out is that they're going to need more money. They're either going to have to get another job, or they're going to be attracted to some type of home-based business opportunity.

Those are the two markets we serve. **Both are only going to get bigger. They're long-term markets; the demand is**

never going to drop, it's only going to increase. It's only going to become more profitable as time goes on. And frankly, teaching people marketing is something that will always need to happen. As long as businesses have existed, they've needed marketing of some kind. Back when it was just word of mouth, they had to learn how to do word of mouth marketing effectively. As we get more technologically advanced, the way we market changes. **Things evolve, but we still need people to teach us how to market effectively.**

A lot of business owners are good at whatever they do for example, if a person is a plumber, they know how to plumb. But they probably don't know how to market. If someone's an electrician, they know how to work with wires and electricity. But do they know how to market their business? As long as business exists, people will need to learn how to market their services and products, and that's what we can teach them through our coaching programs — and, of course, our flagship product, the Wealth Explosion Seminars, where we teach marketing strategies live in front of people. **Companies like ours that teach people how to sell will thrive, because we'll always have plenty of people out there to buy the products and services we sell.**

Selling and marketing are the most important things in any business, and of course, everyone wants to make more money. Small business owners especially can really benefit by learning marketing and mastering sales, because that's the ticket to increased profits, sales, and revenues. And so, it's a perfect message-to-market match, because business owners love to hear you say, "Hey, I'd like to show you how to raise your sales and profits." They want to know that information; **they *need* to know that information,** because without it, they'll struggle or go out of business.

With CLUB-20 International, you're tied in with a

company that knows how to get that word out to that marketplace. You've got to know and understand that marketplace, and all false modesty aside, we do. In a sense, I *am* my ideal customer, because I've lived and breathed this market for a long time, and I was a marketing fanatic long before I hit it big. So it's a great marriage, being able to come together here and profit from all the knowledge and understanding that my colleagues and I have of the marketplace and all the infrastructure we have in place. We've been working with opportunity seekers for a long time, and it takes one to know one. **We understand that market. Plus, we're small business owners too, and we understand the heart and soul of what that's all about.**

Okay, time for Question <u>NUMBER</u> <u>TEN</u> in our twelve-question Acid Test Formula. This question is: **Can the opportunity produce automatic income?**

When I speak of automatic income, **I'm talking about** *residual* **income — money that just comes rolling in month after month.** This is money that has nothing to do with the amount of time and effort that you spend making it. **If there's no automatic income in an opportunity, stay away from it, at least until you're a more seasoned marketer.** You've got to have some kind of automatic income, whether it comes from the continuity of a monthly fee from your subscribers, or because other people are selling your items for you. Subscriptions, for example, are based on products or services that are sold on a till-forbid basis. That's where somebody just signs up, and they make a decision once — but it's an automatic re-purchase. The subscription fee may run as little as a few bucks a month, but some people are charging as much as $1,000 a month for some products and services, particularly high-end coaching programs.

Residual income may also be the result of being able to replicate your business model effectively. This may involve

47

making money off the efforts of other people by means of a sales team like you get when you work with CLUB-20 International. **But it's also a function of good advertising.** For example, if you mail a thousand sales letters and get back a certain percentage of orders, that's automated income. You're not relying on yourself. Whereas if you're a salesperson and have to pick up the phone and call people, you have to do all that work yourself.

So ideally, you're looking for some way to make automatic money without direct effort. That goes back to some of the other things I've talked about already, like how you're spending your time. If you have to be directly involved in every sale, that takes a lot of time and energy. You want to free your time to live the lifestyle you want, so you need some way to make automatic income. **What I look for are things that are going to allow me to plug into an automatic marketing system that's going to put money in my pocket, and then other people's time can go into effect to put money in my pocket when they, too, plug into the same marketing system, so that as** *they* **enjoy success, they build my residual monthly income.** When you have those two principles together in an automated marketing system that people can plug in to, you have the ability to continually produce income from work you had no direct hand in performing. That's when it really becomes powerful.

Let me illustrate this with a short anecdote about a buddy of my colleague Kent Sayre. This fellow basically sells land through mail order. He'll go out and find a plot of land, and he'll pay cash for it and then finance it. That is, he'll sell it on payments to people. When Kent got started in his business, he says, he just wanted to make lump sums of cash, while his friend was strictly focused on automatic income. Kent would always have to work hard, and he'd get a huge sum of money coming in occasionally, so it was feast or famine. If he took it easy one month because he had a good early month, his income would go down. It would be up and down, up and down, up and down... hills and valleys. But his friend focused on automatic income, and this was the thing that made all the difference. His income was steady; he kept getting recurring payments. He never asked for a lump sum and never wanted the land paid off. He just wanted recurring payments, and eventually he grew his passive income to where it's now about a half a million dollars a month — and this guy is semi-retired. These contracts are for 10 years apiece. So for all this land he sold, he's going to have $500,000 coming in every month for the next 10 years — and that makes a *big* difference. It's automatic income, and it can make you massively wealthy. Once Kent saw this, of course, he got hooked on automatic income. Now every opportunity he joins has to have automatic income.

CLUB-20 International is fully automated and ongoing, because that's really the only effective way to make big money. Even better, most of it comes from other people. I've already mentioned repeatedly the $1,000 you get paid every time we help one of your team members make an automated sale. It doesn't get any more automatic than that! You could literally use our automated system to build up a team of distributors and then "retire" and stop selling altogether. In theory, you could work hard for the next 6-12 months to build up a good team and then stop doing anything — no more finding leads, no more selling. Let's say you'd built up a team of a hundred people over that year. You'd get $1,000 each time we help one of those people make a sale. Well, what if all 100 of those people sold one seminar ticket a month? That's $100,000 a month you'd be making! If they just make one sale a year, you could enjoy a steady income of $100,000 a year.

Clearly, the potential for you to make automatic money is tremendous. How much you make depends on several factors, particularly how much you use our system and how much the people we bring into your team use the system. There are a lot of variables, **but the potential to make automatic income is *definitely* available with CLUB-20.** Something that I'm especially proud of is the fact that **our sales team is very good at what they do.** How good are they? Well, we just started promoting our initial August 2009 event in March 2009, and it's June 2009 as I write this. As of this writing, the sales team has already sold more than 200 sales — in just three months.

Once that first event is over, we'll be planning and selling the second event, which will be in San Diego, California. **We're expecting this to be an annual event right now, with as many as several thousand people attending.** That's an arena-sized crowd. If it takes off like we hope it will, maybe we'll change it to two or three times a year. **The point is, we can do anything we want with it, if this thing grows as big as we think it could.** Of course, not everybody who gets involved in the opportunity will want to actually attend the events — so we have the ability to work with people even if they can't come. We have coaching programs available, for example. Those are additional opportunities for you to make money, where we work with people on a more hands-on basis. **Our goal is to help you make as much money as possible through all the different products and services we have available.**

My goal is to eventually fill Carnegie Hall, by the way. I won't be happy until we actually do it. Look, we're excited about this thing! All of us who are involved are just so pumped up about it. **Remember: the same salespeople who are making sales for us are making sales for you.** We've already told you that they don't know whether they're pursuing a lead from the company or a lead from the distributors. We did it that way on purpose, because we want them to work just as hard for you as they work for us. The more money you make, the more money *we* make. As they say, "A rising tide lifts all boats." It's the ideal win-win situation.

Question NUMBER ELEVEN in our Acid Test Formula is: **Is it easy to start?**

Unfortunately, most opportunities *aren't* easy to start, and getting started is the hardest part. **But if you can find an opportunity that's easy to get started in, you've got the power of momentum working for you.** If it takes too much to get started, then you've expended all your energy and resources before you take in your first dollar **so you want something that's fast, simple, and easy.** This "easy to start" aspect is one of the most important ones on our list. Too often, people get vapor locked when they're looking at getting started. They've got an opportunity in front of them. Maybe they've got a start-up package of some kind, or maybe they don't even have that. Maybe all they've got is a little bit of information. In either case, the first question they have is almost always, "What do I do to get started? What do I do to go from here to actually making it do what I want it to do, which is provide me with a life-long income and make millions of dollars? What do I do to get this thing rolling?" That's the big question on everybody's mind.

If you don't have an easy way to get started… well, you stay stopped. You don't ever get going. **So you've got to have some kind of an easy system in place to jump-start the opportunity.** Do they give you an A-B-C, 1-2-3 type of system that says outright, "Here's what to do right now to get started?" What kind of start-up materials do they give you? Do they have a start-up manual, or did they just throw you a few pieces of paper that give you basic information, and then it's up to you to figure it all out? Hopefully not — you've got to have some simple way of getting off to a hot start! **The more an opportunity provider can give you to help you get off to that hot start, the more money you can make and the sooner you**

can make it.

To some extent, this goes back to the support and guidance I discussed before. Has the start-up procedure for someone just coming into the opportunity been thought through in order to determine the best way to get them up and making money? Is it *easy* for someone to get up and get going? If the answer is "No!", then it's failed this part of the Acid Test Formula. If it's "Yes!", then you can move forward.

It's vital that the opportunity be easy to start, because as the Law of Inertia points out, "An object at rest tends to stay at rest, an object in motion tends to stay in motion." If you're at rest, it might take you a little effort to get going. Think about a rocket launch. We've all seen the Space Shuttle take off; it requires a huge amount of thrust built up by the jets to get it off the ground and up into orbit. But once you're *in* orbit, things are relatively easy. Well, the escape velocity required to break free of inertia is what sinks most business opportunities. **If something is hard to start, it's not going to be a successful business opportunity for most people; it's going to be DOA.**

But with CLUB-20 International, we've already got the rocket packets ready for you. In fact, we're launching your rocket for you. Basically, you're just along for the ride, and once you're up here in orbit, it's so easy you're going to love it. It's like a franchise: a tremendous amount of resources, time and effort went into the whole thing in advance, so it's a snap for you to get started. **There's basically just one thing that you, as a distributer, have to do — and that's to generate the leads.** The leads are the people who raise their hand and say, "Yes, send me your free book. Here's my $5 for shipping and handling." **That's how simple it is.** It's based on the same marketing system we've been using since 1988 to generate over $100 million in sales. It works!

And this is a great offer. **Not only do they get the free book, but they also get a free entry-level position in CLUB-20.** Now we can speak to them as distributors. They're not just people who sent for a free book; they're part of the organization. That means we can proceed to work with them and show them how it's in their best interests to go ahead and purchase the flagship product, which eliminates the qualification period and gets them into the commissions fast — which is what they want anyway.

The product is completely guaranteed. We're looking for the best distributors for you and for us, so we're in it together. It's as easy as mailing out a simple postcard or writing some classified ads — and *we* can mail the postcards for you if you want, using our 5-Star Mailing System. Now, let me discuss that with you a bit. **Our 5-Star Mailing System takes the automation even further, letting you work with the same suppliers we've worked with for many, many years.** Those suppliers help us with all our printing and mailing. So if, for example, we have a postcard we need to mail, and we've got a group of 1,000 people we want to mail it to, we can go to our printer, give them the postcard layout, and they'll print it up for us. Then it goes to our mailing house, where it will be personalized with the names and addresses of the people on our list. They do all the customization. They barcode them, do all the special things that get the best rates from the post office, sort them based on the regions of the U.S. they're going to, put the stamps on them, then deliver them to the post office. Our mailing house and our printer are invaluable resources to us, so we decided to make them available to our clients.

When you get involved with our 5-Star Mailing System, you can let our suppliers print and mail postcards to advertise the free book for you. It's a monthly service, so you don't have to worry about it at all. Consider it your ad agency, or your entire marketing system if you want to. You can tell them that you'd like them to print and mail anywhere from 500 to 2,000 postcards a month, and it will be done automatically. You don't have to worry about it. **Or you can choose the self-service option.** If you have your own mailing list, or if you have another way to advertise and just want to drop the postcards into your packages as you send them out, you can order postcards custom-printed for you and delivered to you.

If you'd rather we just do everything for you, we'll print your cards, rent mailing lists, do all the customization and personalization, and mail them for you every month. **You don't have to worry about *anything*.** They can print your website address right on them, so anybody who gets that card in the mail can go right to your website and fill out the order form. They pay the $5 to us, and we send them the book. Again, because we merge those leads with all our other leads, they get a call from our sales department, they get mailings where we explain the opportunity to them, and they're able to sign up for their seminar ticket. So that's another automated system we have in place for you.

The people handling our 5-Star Mailing System are the same suppliers we've been using for years — since 1990 — in the case of **our mailing house, CCI out of Wichita, Kansas** (CCI stands for Contemporary Communications, Incorporated). They're an honest company. We found them because the company we were using previously *wasn't* honest, so we shopped around until we found someone who was. They're a great company. They mail out millions of pieces of Direct-Mail for us every year, and now they mail out pieces for all of our clients who are involved in this opportunity. **Our printer is City Print out of Wichita, Kansas;** we've been with them since 1994. Again, a great company; I can't say enough good things about them. We shopped around for many different printers before we found them; we even had our own little printing company for a while. It was an in-house project that became a major disaster for us.

So you're working with the same suppliers we're working with. They do a really great job. They get pieces out on time, they're very reasonable in pricing; and they're very professional. They're of the highest quality. I feel so strongly about that, that I've passed the contact information for both CCI and City Print on to a lot of my friends in the business over the years. And these friend used CCI and City Print, and then they told a few of their marketing friends about those two companies, and then they told a few of *their* friends and a few of *their* friends... and just like when you throw a big brick in the middle of a pond, there was a ripple effect. Now, Wichita may be the biggest city in Kansas, but it's still pretty small compared to a city like Dallas or Chicago. But here in Wichita, you can walk into City Print or CCI, and you'll see that they have hundreds of other marketing customers. It's because they're honest; they're dependable; they do what they say; they say what they do; and they're reasonably priced. And word gets out.

I think it's pretty cool how, back in the mid-1990s, my wife and I recommended them to less than 20 people. That's how it started — almost like MLM, although we haven't gotten paid a dime for this stuff! Back then, we belonged to this little organization run by Dan Kennedy, that met several times a year. There were about 18 of us, and we went and bragged to all of the people in that little group, "Hey, you guys ought to use this company." And now they're getting business from hundreds of marketers, from all over the country. Hey, I think we should get free printing and mailing for life!

Seriously, it's a reciprocal relationship; we help each other. Take our printer: he used to be just a regular printer, and now he's almost exclusively a Direct-Response printer. He knows the business so well that he can suggest different papers to us, different envelopes we could use — because he's done so much in the industry for so many people. And not just people in *our* marketplace, but people who sell all kinds of products to all kinds of industries. He's got clients in the furniture industry, the carpet cleaning industry, and all kinds of retail service businesses. He can show us samples of what other people are using, and we can spy on people like Kent Sayre and Chris Hollinger! We know what they're doing before it even goes out in the mail stream, and of course we have the advantage of working with a printer who's an expert in Direct-Response.

This allows us an advantage over working with a printer who just does printing and happens to also be working with us. **To draw this back to CLUB-20, what that means is that he helps us help you as well, because he knows all the tricks of the trade.** You might be surprised to learn that just an eighth of an inch difference in size can sometimes make the difference in the postage jumping up 20 or 30 cents. So he'll tell us to trim our postcard down a little bit, or maybe make it a little bigger. Or he'll say, "Hey, if you do this kind of postcard, you can save some money, and you don't really lose any space." So working with Steve at City Print and working with Pam at CCI, our mailing house, helps us... **but it also helps you, because we can get you guys the best prices.**

Let's say you wanted to mail 500 postcards a month. Well, if you just came into the mailing house from off the street and told them you wanted to mail 500 postcards, first of all, they'd probably laugh at you and tell you that's too small a volume. They deal in large volumes; they can't work with small quantities like that. But if you work with 20 or 30 other people doing 500 or 1,000 pieces each, that starts adding up in quantity. So not only are they able to work with you, but they pass along volume-based price savings to you, because they might be printing 20,000, 30,000, 40,000, or 50,000 postcards for a bunch of clients all at the same time. **Then our mailing house can give you some savings, because they're doing their processes in bulk, so it all actually ends up saving you money.**

If you were to go to your own printer and mailing house and you were to say, "Here, I want you to print and mail these 500 or 1,000 pieces for me," and you got the price for everything — including printing, postage, the mailing list, etc.— and then were to compare that with what you're paying through us... well, you're going to get significant savings with us. Now, there may be a situation where that's not the case, but generally speaking that's going to be the rule.

And here's the <u>LAST</u> <u>QUESTION</u> in our 12-point litmus test: **Is there an exit strategy, in case something goes wrong or in case you just want out?**

That's the one thing most people never ask themselves. They get caught up in the excitement and never ask about the exit strategy. **The ultimate exit strategy is always a bank full of money, because that's power.** Whenever you've got that, you can quit anytime you want. Many business owners are stuck, though. **You've got to look for a business you can sell, or otherwise get out of whenever you're ready.** Because with most businesses, the only simple exit strategy is death. Some businesspeople *do* kill themselves, because they can't handle it when things go wrong.

A lot of distributors in MLM will spend years building a huge downline, so now they're making $20,000, $30,000 or $50,000 a month, and they're living this super-high lifestyle where they're spending almost all of it. And then, all of a sudden, something happens to the company — and their income goes out the window. **So you absolutely have to think through the exit strategies, so you can protect yourself in case things go sour.**

My best friend has a pest control business, and one of the reasons she got into the business to begin with is because it's got a really great exit strategy. Those companies are extremely salable; she can sell anytime she wants. In fact, she has standing offers right now to sell. Anytime she wants to sell the business, it's a phone call away. That's just one example of an excellent exit strategy... **but most people never think about getting out, and they should think about that before they get in.**

You always tend to think, "Well, it's going to be successful. Why would I ever want to get out?" But there are any number of reasons — some foreseeable and others that aren't — that could cause you to need to back out of a business or opportunity. It could have nothing to do with whether you're successful with it or not — issues with family members or health can derail you, for example. There are all kinds of reasons why you would need to get out of a business; thus, you need to look for one that's easy to exit if that should become necessary. Even if you start a regular retail business like a pest control company, ask yourself, "Is it salable? Can I dump this quickly if I need to? If I need to back out, step down, if something comes up — a family emergency, or whatever — and I just need to absolve myself of this responsibility, what can I do to back out?"

So you want to make sure it's salable, or that you can somehow get rid of it easily, or turn it over to somebody else. Think about how it ends for you. If you'll consider that, even just abstractly, it puts you in a position of authority and power going into the situation. The worst thing you want is to be in a position where you have to dump it quickly, so you get rid of it for far less value than it's worth. It's sort of like moving real estate or a car. The more you have to sell it, the lower the price gets, because everybody knows you're desperate. You want to think about these things ahead of time.

From the very beginning, you need to test the "what ifs"

and "just in case" scenarios that you typically don't *want* to consider going into a brand new opportunity. It's a wise business move to be able to say, "Okay, should this happen, this is what I can do." **Having good value at the end makes you happier about the decision to get into it in the first place.** That's one thing that distinguishes sophisticated entrepreneurs: they always begin with an end in mind, an escape hatch they can climb out of if necessary. For a lot of entrepreneurs, it's all about selling their company and getting the monster payday. That's when you get to cash-in on all the equity and value you've created. Good entrepreneurs do think of exit strategies when they enter into anything.

Partnerships, for example. One of the most important things to consider when getting into a partnership is having an exit strategy. When a partnership goes sour, when partners are fighting, that's the worst time for them to discuss how to separate things. It's kind of like an acrimonious divorce. But when you're getting in, and you can see the exit strategy, you see the light at the end of the tunnel.

What's so exciting about CLUB-20 International is that there are exit strategies in place for you, something you very rarely find in other business opportunities. Because it's not a traditional MLM company, there's no heavy downline being built; and therefore, the distributors are getting paid up-front very quickly. Even if something bad were to happen with our company, you still get paid. We're not going to leave you holding the bag with all these extra commissions.

We deal with so many clients who are involved in MLM — and many such companies are infamous for firing their best distributors. These are distributors who go out and give it everything they've got. They put years of their lives into these companies. They build huge downlines, and then the companies either go out of business — sometimes for regulatory reasons, and sometimes because the guys at the top just take the money and run — or the companies get tired of paying those guys $50,000 and $100,000 a month, so they find reasons to can them.

And so the poor guy's screwed. He's worked hard, and made all this money, and he's dependent on it. And then something goes wrong, and he's out on his rear — without an exit strategy. There's some legal recourse, maybe, but it sometimes takes years of legal fees to work it out, and those established companies often have better legal staffs than most people can afford.

The exit strategy for CLUB-20 International is simple. We're not a traditional MLM company. We pay the largest commissions to the fewest number of distributors. Therefore, there's no money that we're holding back from you. People get paid quickly. **Every time we make a sale for you or a distributor, the money goes out immediately. Right there is exit strategy enough.**

So what happens if you face the worst-case scenario and you die? Are you able to pass the business along to a member of your family or a business partner? **Well, with CLUB-20, yes, you *can* transfer the business.** If you're bringing in a lot of money every month, you don't want that to just stop because you died. You want to pass that on! You want it to be a part of your estate! And with CLUB-20 International, it can be.

That's worst-case scenario, but there are other cases. Suppose you have to leave the country; are you able to take the business with you? What about if you get ill, and you can't run the business anymore; can someone else take it over for you? Or can you still make money even if you're sick and you can't actually do anything? **Well, we have passive income ability here, so it doesn't matter if you're ill.**

With a lot of businesses, you have to be actively involved to make money. If you're a salesperson out on the road every day, and you hurt your back and can't drive, well, what do you do? You either have someone else drive you around so you can go sell your stuff, or you're out of action and you can't sell. Those are the kinds of things you want to think through. With CLUB-20, not only do we have passive income with our automated system, but there are options available to you if something happens and you have to back out, step down, or — even worse — you die. **There are things that can happen so that either you or your next of kin could continue earning income from the business.**

We actually had this happen recently. We learned from a client's family that our client had died about a month before, and they were asking if they could continue getting the commission checks that the client had been getting. Of course there's some legal stuff to work through here, but we're going to be able to continue paying commissions to the family of this client who passed on. So yes, that kind of thing does happen — and it's something you have to at least consider. What happens in this scenario? With most opportunities, you're out. It's for you and you alone. **But CLUB-20 has a specific strategy in place where you're able to pass this on to someone else.** A business that's willable and saleable is always the best-case scenario, and that's what you have here.

We've just run through the twelve points of the Acid Test Formula that we use when considering a new opportunity, the 12 questions that we ask ourselves first. **Now, there are plenty of other items we consider, but they all relate back to these 12 in one way or another.** Remember, this is what we use to analyze *every* business opportunity we investigate. Most opportunities can never make it past the first three questions. Heck, most opportunities can't make it past the *first* question!

This allows us to look at hundreds of opportunities every year and just say, "Nope. Nope. Yes. Maybe. No. No." Because after all, you've got to have a way of separating the wheat from the chaff, the sheep from the goats. This formula is why we're able to get through so many opportunities so quickly. Usually we'll know whether it's worthwhile just by looking over the first three questions — it never goes on to the fourth.

Let me just remind you what those first three questions are. FIRST of all, if average people aren't making money already, if only the heavy hitters or only the people who have a lot of knowledge and experience are getting rich, then forget it. Just move on to something else. **We're especially looking for opportunities where average people are not only making money, but they're making it in spite of certain mistakes they're making.** When we see things like that we get really excited, because then all you have to do is fix the mistakes and you can make even *more* money. So if average people are making money already, that's great!

Number TWO is, can it be started for about the money that you'd spend for a good used car? If it's going to cost a hundred grand, forget it. I told you about my best friend and her pest control business. What I didn't tell you is she spent about $575,000 to buy that company. We wouldn't ever recommend something like that to our clients.

And then the THIRD question is, is it possible to make thousands of dollars right away? With a lot of companies it takes time to get to that point. You've got to develop your customer base, and too many things can go wrong in the interim. We're not interested in those types of opportunities.

Consider franchise opportunities, where the parent company has spent an enormous amount of time, work, effort, energy, and money to develop the flagship operations required before they can start selling the franchises. Those are the kinds of opportunities you should look for. They're substantial, they've got proven track records, and the companies involved make big profits. In fact, that's how they make *all* their profits — by collecting a piece of every dollar they help their franchisees make. **CLUB-20 is something new, but it contains all the characteristics of a good franchise opportunity.**

In this book, **I'm going to cover 53 more points that characterize a good opportunity and tell you how CLUB-20 International meets those criteria.** This is only the first chapter, but a lot of the themes that I've talked about in this first session will reappear in others. Again, these are the 12 things that we think are really most important when considering a business opportunity. Now, it doesn't mean that every opportunity has to have all 12 in order to be worth pursuing. But the more of these 12 things the opportunity you're looking at has, the better your chance of success. Does that mean we've jumped into opportunities that didn't have all 12 and have failed at all of them? No. We've been successful at some that didn't have all 12, and we've also failed at some that *did*. So it's not a checklist per se, where if everything works out just like this and all these things are exactly right, then you're guaranteed success. There are too many other variables that go into whether you're going to be successful or not. **But these are the 12 things that we think are key.** And if you can answer "Yes!" to most of these questions, they set you up to give yourself the best chance for success.

That's why we think these 12 things are important. They give you a guideline of things that you can look for when you're evaluating an opportunity — something to go by other than your gut, other than your feelings. This is a point-by-point list of things that you can do to test any business venture or opportunity to see if it measures up. Is it something that you should get involved in and spend your money on? Are people making money with it? And how much does it cost to start? It can really help you make a decision — and frankly, I haven't seen anything like this anywhere else. **I honestly feel that this little Acid Test Formula, which you can apply fairly quickly to any opportunity, can save you thousands of dollars.** Every business opportunity promoter hypes up their business opportunity, but there weren't any objective, almost scientific criteria to judge them by — until now. Not only can this formula save you money by avoiding the wrong opportunities, you'll be able to choose the *right* opportunity to maximize your profit. This can save you a lot of frustration, a lot of money, and a lot of wasted energy and effort.

This is a logical type of thinking process, and most of the decisions that are made when purchasing business opportunities are, frankly, emotional. I've already mentioned that for years I sent away for one program after another. I'd get all excited about a program, and I'd get involved without ever putting in any significant thought on it — without ever putting in any significant time or effort into examining it. I've learned better, and this is my way of passing on this knowledge.

I started this book with our Acid Test Formula for a specific reason, and that's because **you need to get serious only about those opportunities where you can get an affirmative answer on the first three questions.** And then, if you get some "No" answers on the other nine, that's fine. But always, always, *always* stay away from any opportunity where the answers to those first three questions are "No!" That's the best advice I can give you. **Try to get as many "Yes!" answers to the other nine questions as possible,** but realize that most opportunities can never make it past the first three. The next time you're all hyped-up about an opportunity, just ask those first three questions, And if the answer is "No!," then you've spent only a few minutes to save yourself a lot of hassle.

CHAPTER TWO:

The Six Powerful Ingredients

All business involves risk. There's nothing you can do to completely avoid it, **but there *are* things that you can do to minimize it.**

Here's something I thought was funny: my wife once had a success coach, through Tony Robbins' company, and one day she was trying to explain what our business is. When she was done, her coach said, "You know, that just sounds so much like gambling." Well, I suppose to the average person who looks at some of the things we do at M.O.R.E., Inc., it *does* look like gambling! We mail millions of Direct-Mail pieces every year. We don't know exactly how things are going to go. We make all kinds of decisions that involve tens of thousands of dollars before we really know what's going to happen. We make all kinds of commitments and take on obligations before we know what's going on, because yes, a lot of what we do *is* speculative.

To the outsider, it can indeed seem as if it's all just a bunch of gambling — and certainly there have been times when we've lost millions of dollars. **Everybody knows we've *made* millions, but there have been times when we've lost millions, too.** So our system isn't perfect; I don't want to say that it is. We've lost plenty of money. But the thing is, **we do lots of different things to try to minimize the risks.** And that's the secret of the type of thinking that's gone into all 65 of the points I'm presenting in this book. What can you do to minimize your business risk?

In this chapter, I'm going to discuss another formula that we've used for years when testing opportunities. We call it the "Six Powerful Ingredients That You Need to Get Rich." Now, some of these ingredients you've seen before in the Acid Test Formula; the two are closely interrelated, though not identical. However, I believe repetition is good for the soul, so even if I've discussed a particular topic, I'm going to re-emphasize it here in order to help you internalize it. And don't worry — I'll provide some new information, too.

THE FIRST INGREDIENT is one of those items; it should be familiar, because it's basically the same as the first point in the Acid Test Formula. **Many average people must already be making huge sums of money**.

The more average these people are, the more excited you should get. If it's only the heavy hitters at the top making the big bucks, then you should get less excited. You're looking for average people and, specifically, you're looking for average people who are making money in spite of making certain mistakes or doing things haphazardly. **Those are the opportunities that should get you very, *very* excited.** One of the metaphors I like to use is the metaphor of the chain; perhaps you've heard it. You can have the thickest chain that money can buy, something that can pull a farm implement that might weigh many tons, but if just one of those links in that chain is ready to break, then you're in danger. You could lose it all. You could be pulling something that costs hundreds of thousands of dollars with a big semi-truck and with a huge chain, and if just one link in that chain is weak, then there goes your investment. So when we talk about the importance of average people making huge sums of money, I think of that analogy.

How do you find out whether average people are making money? Well, **you've got to do your due diligence, and it all involves working with people that you trust, because you**

can't believe everything you hear. There are plenty of testimonials you'll see where they don't even use the real person's name. It'll be T.K. in Connecticut, or M.R. in Philadelphia. C'mon, now. And even the ones where they provide pictures — those can be stock photographs. You just never know! Recently, Chris Hollinger and his wife were investigating an opportunity and his wife said, "Well, let me see. Who are these testimonials?" They included the person's name and the town they lived in, so she started trying to find them online, trying to see if she could match them up to real people. She Googled them and did some White Pages searches and tried to find them... and she couldn't find a single one. Now, if every single one of their testimonials results in a miss, then there's probably something a little odd there.

One of the neat things about Network Marketing is that you tend to have events that you can go to and do some due diligence and investigative reporting. You can talk to the people attending, ask them questions. This makes Network Marketing a cut above most opportunities. Now, as I've said, CLUB-20 International is based on some opportunities that we got involved with several years ago where we knew some of the people who were making the money, because we had networked with them. **One thing that got us so jazzed about all this was the fact that they were making all kinds of mistakes, but were still doing quite well.** There were three very specific mistakes, which I'll talk about later, where we knew that if we corrected those mistakes, we could make ten times more money than they were making.

CLUB-20 International is based on a type of compensation plan that we first encountered when we got involved with a company out of Panama City, Panama. That company really opened our eyes to a whole new way of making money with the best aspects of Network Marketing — but it wasn't a Network

Marketing opportunity per se. There are a whole lot of companies doing it now; **it's a trend to move away from more traditional MLM and into this other area.** And within all these different companies there are many average people making above-average incomes. The difference is that, again, the distributors are compensated in a way that's the exact opposite of the way that most MLM companies do it. Instead of paying small commissions scattered out over large groups of distributors, **we pay large commissions to small numbers of distributors. That lets people get paid fast; it lets them get momentum going for them.** CLUB-20 is brand new, so we don't have a long history of success to share with you yet, but it's based on what's working well for a lot of people right now. We built this compensation plan around several companies from which we took the best of the best features, one of which made us $100,000 a month. Other people were using that same system to make $50,000 to $100,000 a month.

Incidentally, I want to point out that the fact that you can make such huge amounts of money is going it irritate some people. Chris Hollinger was recently telling me about something that he has an issue with, and that's the idea of "obscene profits." His mother-in-law has a very socialist agenda sometimes, and she's quick to point out that people like teachers and farmers don't get paid enough for what they provide. Maybe so. And yet, why should someone hold it against you when you have a promotional-based income that makes a whole lot more money? The opportunity was there for that person to do that, and to hold something against someone because they're making large profits makes no sense. Ironically Chris was a teacher himself before he moved into the marketing business and started making those "obscene profits"!

It's a touchy subject, especially in this economy. I like the attitude of the head men's basketball coach at the University of

Connecticut, Jim Calhoun. His contracted salary is $1.6 million a year. A reporter asked him, "Don't you think your contract is a little excessive, given today's economic climate?" And his answer was, "The University of Connecticut men's basketball team brings in $12 million a year to the university. Shut up!" You see, profits are only "obscene" when someone else is making them. **If it's *you* making those profits, how obscene are they to you?** They're not obscene at all! And ask yourself: "What good can I do with obscene profits?"

<u>INGREDIENT</u> <u>NUMBER</u> <u>TWO</u>: **You must be able to do everything part-time from the comfort, privacy, and security of your own home.**

This is another one I've talked about in other segments, but I'm emphasizing it again, because it's crucial for you to be able to do things part-time. **One of the big reasons people are looking for a new business to get into is because they want to escape the daily grind of a full-time, 9-to-5 job.** And really, the joke is that the 9-to-5 jobs are mostly gone. Most people are working more than they ever were before. Many times it's not 9-to-5, Monday to Friday anymore; now it's 8-to-6 or 7-to-5 or 7-to-7, and it's Monday through Saturday and Sundays occasionally.

People want to escape that, and so they're looking for opportunities that get them out of that grind and into something more comfortable so they can spend more time with their families. **That's why it's important to be able to pursue an opportunity part-time.** If it takes full-time energy, full-time commitment, in many cases you're not much better off than you were before when you were working for somebody else. **Being able to work from home is important for similar reasons.** You want to be able to control everything. If you have to be out on the road all the time, you don't have the freedom to enjoy spending time with your family. But pick the right opportunity, and if you want to get up in the morning and take a walk with your kid or your spouse, you can do that. If you have a swimming pool in the back yard and you want to go for a swim, you're able to do that. There are benefits to being home. **So not only do you want to look for opportunities that allow you to do everything part-time, but you want to be able to do things from home.** Those are some of the reasons why I think this ingredient is important.

My Dad was never around when I was a kid. He was always on the road, because he was a lawyer, and that's what his job demanded. And what good is something like that? It's no accident that he and my Mom got divorced. You can't do everything if you're always gone. **So it's good to find these opportunities that give you the freedom to build your business around your life instead of vice versa, as is so often the case.** With CLUB-20 International, you're using our marketing system to give away that valuable book that's sold on Amazon.com, Barnesandnoble.com, and other places online for $19.95. You don't have to travel, or have your own office, or work 80 hours a week.

What do we consider part-time? **Well, that's subjective.** I'd say that if you're using our automated marketing system with our 5-Star Mailing Service, it might be as little as 10 minutes a day. Again, you're getting paid on the sale of the products and services. You're letting the marketing system make the sales for you, so there's very little work here. But you could put in a lot more time if you wanted to, of course. And it doesn't matter where you are when you do it; you could do it on vacation.

The big secret here is that you're making money on things other than the time you put in. Of course, if you tell most people that they can make lots of money working as little as 10 minutes a day, they're going to think, "Oh man, this is a scam! You guys are scamming me. There has *got* to be something wrong here." But that's not the case. **You're getting**

paid on the sales that our marketing system makes for you, and remember, you're also getting paid the same amount of commission on the sales that our marketing system makes for the people we automatically place into your team.

INGREDIENT NUMBER THREE: **The market for your products and services must be *huge* and growing quickly. There must be a genuine demand for the items you offer.**

Obviously, you don't want to be in a situation where it's up to you to create the demand for your product. **You want that demand to be there, to be a part of that exploding trend.** Again, positioning yourself in front of that growing trend and having everything ready so that you can capitalize on the trend is crucial. Now, I know we keep picking on Network Marketing, but with so many of their products there's no true demand — there's only the excitement or hype that's generated on conference calls and sales events to get people to believe in that product. If you get yourself involved with a product or a service that doesn't have genuine demand, you've got to be a super-salesman to make ends meet, because it's like pushing a wet noodle uphill. That's not to say that some people can't make those sales, because some certainly can. But if there's a huge demand for the product or services you have to offer, then it makes your job a lot easier, and it makes whatever marketing systems are in place on your behalf a lot more effective.

The bigger the market and the faster it's growing, the more opportunities there are within it. That's where the money is, where the opportunity lies, so look for markets that are part of growing trends. Look for markets where the demand is huge! Those are the ones with the largest potential opportunity. **You have to find "hot" markets;** that's the main thing. Where are other people making huge sums of money?

If people just aren't interested in an opportunity, then no

matter how hard you try, and no matter what level your salesmanship is, you're not going to sell them. It doesn't matter if you're a world-class salesman or not — you can't sell somebody something they absolutely aren't interested in. Let me give you an example: if somebody tried to sell me gold-plated knitting needles, nothing would work. They might send me the world's greatest sales letter. They might have a 30-step follow-up campaign to sell me those needles, but I'm just not going to be interested in them — ever. There's not a demand there.

You want to enter into the conversation the prospects are already having in their own minds. You want to use your marketing systems to fan that spark of desire into a wildfire, because *that's* when people will buy. And that's what a good marketing system will do. That's why our opportunity is so important. **We serve two markets that both have serious demands — demands that *must* be met.** These are demands that other people are filling right now with non-MLM companies and distributor-based operations. A wide variety of products and services are being sold very successfully by a number of different companies to both of these two markets, because they're tapping into the huge and growing demand I've talked about. There's a giant marketplace of people who are interested in making more money, and there's also a huge number of businesses that need coaching and marketing help and need to learn what we have to teach. It's music to the ears of every business owner when you tell them you've got a way for them to make money that their competition doesn't know about. Give them a competitive advantage and help them kick their competition's butts, and they're going to love you. All business owners are looking for that type of thing. Plus, many people have thought about selling through home-based businesses, so those are the markets that we serve. **There's a huge demand.**

And here's INGREDIENT NUMBER FOUR: **The items**

being offered must be high-ticket products and services that pay you the largest sum of money for the smallest number of transactions.

This is crucial, because high-ticket items are automatically going to have a bigger built-in profit margin. **It's easier to make a million dollars with a thousand transactions at $1,000 each than it is trying to sell a million people for a dollar.** You might think, "Oh, if I could just get a million people to just give me a dollar, I'd be a millionaire! Well, sure, but actually, it's easier to sell 1,000 people a $1,000 transaction size. If somebody's predisposed to buying it and you've got a world-class marketing system backing it to fan the flames of their desire, it's not a thousand times more difficult. When you realize this and start selling bigger ticket items, your business will shoot through the roof, because you start making more profit per transaction.

And another thing: if you're just going around selling low-margin and low-profit stuff, you have a lot more customers to service. If you sell a few higher ticket items you may not have a huge customer base, but you're going to make more profit. **The customer is going to be more committed because they've spent more money — and I think you're going to create a better customer.** That's one thing you want to do with every transaction. Every marketer has stories about customers who bought small-ticket items, then turned out to be more demanding than customers who spent thousands. If I had $1,000 right now for every time this has happened, I'd have millions of dollars on my hands. We've had some really irate customers, people who become customer service nightmares, but when we looked at their buying history, we found that they'd hardly brought anything from us. In some cases, they were just leads who never even bought *anything*!

So it's really important that you sell high-ticket products and services or have a marketing system that does that for you.

You just make the most amount of money that way. Whether a thousand people give you $1,000 or a hundred people give you $10,000, it all adds up to a million. Our goal is a million a month, and we've got charts hanging up all over the place that show us exactly what we have to do to make that goal. It's based not only on how many sales we make, but on various average price points and the level of conversions that we need to achieve those numbers. It's *so* much easier to sell big-ticket items. It's hard to get rich without them. **And if you have a high-ticket item, it allows you to spend more money to break each sale.** If you're looking at marketing and advertising costs, it lets you say, "Okay, I'm going to be able to do this many follow-ups to really build their desire for this, because I've got enough margin here that I can do more things in my marketing and advertising to attract more people and to convert more sales of the people that I do attract." **You can definitely outspend all of your competitors.**

The secret is simple: **stay away from opportunities that offer low-ticket items,** unless those can become secondary business opportunities for you and not your primary opportunity. Now, I think you can see that the answer we're offering is very clear. **We're paying $1,000 on our flagship product, our three-day Wealth Explosion Seminar.** We're paying even more than that on some of the coaching programs we sell.

Again, high-ticket items are important because of the ability to recover your marketing costs. Giving away the free book doesn't make you any money; you make money when someone buys the product. And having a high-ticket item brings in the profit quickly, which is kind of the whole point. A lot of people working with MLM companies are selling juices, pills, and other lower-end products, stuff that might sell for $20-$30, and you keep just a small amount of that. There's not any big profit there. With big-ticket items like our seminar — where you get paid $1,000 on every sale — and our coaching programs, you'll get you where you want to be more quickly. **We specialize in high-ticket items, serving a specialty marketplace, and that means that you have the ability to make a lot of money with just one sale.** So if you need a little extra pocket money some month, go out, use our system, and sell one seminar, and we'll send you a $1,000. It doesn't take a lot of sales to make big money.

INGREDIENT NUMBER FIVE: **You've got to have the help, support, and guidance of people who truly understand how to turn small sums of money into a huge fortune.** And on top of that, these people have to earn the bulk of their money by doing everything they can to help you get rich.

That fits us to a T. In the beginning, we merged the best of two programs — George Hoskins' in Montreal and Laser Phase out of Chicago — to form our first product, *Dialing For Dollars*, a unique program that took off like a rocket. Both those companies made their money by helping other people make money. That's why we did well with both of those programs before we merged them to create our own program. There are so many opportunities out there where the only thing they make their money off of is the sale of the product or service. **They have no vested interest in helping you whatsoever, and those are the deals to stay away from.**

You need to find companies who will be your partners, so even if you're in business for yourself, you're never *by* yourself. If you want to get somewhere, or if you want to get ahead and make more money than you're making now, consider this: who do you talk to? Who do you hang out with? Well, you don't want to hang out with people who are making less money than you. You don't want to hang out with people who haven't even figured out as much as you have. **You want to hang out with and learn from people who've done more than you, who've made more**

money than you, who've been more successful than you. This is all part of the guidance, help, and support concept.

Who do you look to as a mentor in business? If all you ever hear is your family and your friends telling you you're crazy to think you can get into your own business and be successful — that you should just stick to having a day job, or you should just give up on your dream of ever being successful — you need to get away from them. They're a major influence on your ability to succeed. On the flip side, if you spend your time listening to people who say, "Hey, you can do it, because I've done it! Look what I've done! See, here's my system. I'll give it to you. Look, you can do exactly what I did!"—well, that's a positive influence, so there's no reason to think you can't do it. And if there's positive reinforcement, then you're constantly looking up instead of down. **Who you get help, support, and guidance from really can set the stage for your success.** It's important to look to people who've been where you're trying to go.

And what happens is, their success is tied to your success, so they've got a self-interest. They're motivated to make more money. You get just such support with CLUB-20 International. At M.O.R.E., Inc., our parent company, we truly do understand how to turn small sums of money into a huge fortune. That's our basic story, after all; we started with just $300. Why only $300? Because, quite simply, that's all we had! And to get that $300, we had to sell a 1985 six-cylinder Chevy van that ran only on five of its cylinders and smoked everywhere it went. It was one of my carpet cleaning trucks, and it was a piece of junk. But somebody gave me a few hundred bucks for it, and that's the money we used to start our company. We've learned how to shoestring money. **Somebody can only teach you what they know — and we have a lot of experience with that.**

The second part of INGREDIENT NUMBER FIVE is: **These people must earn a bulk of their money by doing**

everything they can to help you get rich. Again, you're dealing with skepticism. If someone's interesting in getting involved with your opportunity, they want to know what's in it for you. Why are you willing to make this available? We've heard some variation of this hundreds of times: "If this is such a great moneymaking opportunity, why not keep it for yourself? What's in it for you to help me?"

And with some opportunities, the answer is, "Well, I don't know." But *we* make money when we help *you* make money. We make an average of $1,000 for every $1,000 we can help put in your pocket. So do the math: right now, our Wealth Explosion Seminar sells for about $3,000. We have a $1,000-off discount; the normal price is $4,000, but we're selling it now for $3,000. (If you're reading this sometime in the future, our price may be different.) So when you sell a seminar ticket, you get $1,000. If you someone on your team sells one, they would get $1,000 and you get the same. That's $2,000, so there's about $1,000 left over for us to cover our expenses and make a profit. Therefore, **we're making approximately the same amount of money we're paying you.** It's simple math, easy to understand, and that's *why* it's in our best interest to do everything we can to help you make money. If we have a small army of affiliates and distributors out there, of course we're making a lot of money by helping you, and we can make so much more than we would be able to make all by ourselves.

In our time, we've sold millions of dollars worth of seminars and millions of dollars worth of coaching programs just for ourselves; **so it's clear we know what we're doing.** If there's one thing I don't like it's a hypocrite, somebody who tells you what to do, but then doesn't follow that advice. I assure you, we're no hypocrites. **We've got the experience, and we have a vested interest in helping you, because we're rewarded for making sure *you* are rewarded.**

Finally, <u>INGREDIENT</u> <u>NUMBER</u> <u>SIX</u>: **Does the opportunity have a marketing system, or better, an automated marketing system that does all the selling for you?**

I've already touched on this several times. **The big problem with a lot of opportunities is that there's nothing figured out.** You don't know how you're supposed to make it work, how you're supposed to sell the product. Maybe they give you the rights to the product; well, in some cases, you can spend a lot of money acquiring those rights, and then it's up to you to figure out what you do from there. How do you go about selling it? How are you making money? Do they give you a website, or do you build your own? Do they give you any ad copy, or do you have to write that? Do they give you *anything*?

My Marketing Director Chris Lakey was recently working with a guy who has a business selling customized Information Technology (IT). He'll basically become your IT department. He works with small companies who need their computer networks administered and backed up. When Chris asked him what kind of marketing materials he got from the company that supplies all the software and such, the guy basically said, "Uh, none." So he's probably licensing the rights to represent this software and to be able to set it up for people, and I'm guessing he probably pays a substantial fee for those rights. But he has no marketing system, so he needs help to figure out how to market it.

That's the way it is with a lot of things. **You want to focus on opportunities that have some kind of automated marketing system in place,** so you can spend your time just handling the business and enjoying the fruits of your labor. You don't want to spend a lot of time trying to figure things out, or building a marketing system yourself.

One of the reasons we offer this automatic marketing system is because we know how hard it is for the average new entrepreneur to ask for the money. **So you need a marketing system that consistently asks for the money on your behalf.** If you consistently ask for the money in the right way, people are going to consistently say, "Yes, yes, yes!" And then when they do say "No!" you ask them again. A good marketing system can do those types of things for you, and that's the big difference between this and personal selling. Now, I've known some phenomenal personal salesman; they could sit down and sell anything to anybody. But they couldn't duplicate themselves easily, **whereas a marketing system can be duplicated indefinitely.** This can be the difference between success and failure for some people, because it's the system that consistently asks for the money, not the individual. The marketing system also needs to be easy to scale up; that is, if it works on a small scale, it needs to work on a large scale, too. If for every 1,000 letters mailed you can turn out $100 profit, and you can do this consistently, then it's just a matter of how many names you can get your hands on and roll out to.

In order to have that, all you need is the sales materials and the contacts. To me, a marketing system reminds me of when I was a kid, when we used to watch the Ed Sullivan Show every Sunday night (and I know that dates me a little!). I remember how I was so fascinated when, on more than one occasion, I saw the plate spinner. They'd set up these rods in a row and they'd get one plate spinning, and then they'd go and get another plate spinning, and another, and they'd just keep walking back and forth, spinning these plates. They'd just barely tap them one after another to keep them spinning; so all they had to do was keep walking along slowly, tapping each plate, to keep these giant rows of plates spinning forever! Everything was fine as long as the plates keep getting tapped every once in a while. That's how a marketing system is to me. **It's automatic; you start it up, and it just keeps going with very little maintenance.** I never forgot that lesson.

Our CLUB-20 International marketing system literally does all the selling for you, because we recognize that without a proper marketing system, your business is always going to be nothing but a roller coaster. You're going to have some good months, and you're going to have some bad months. It's going to be feast or famine. **But this marketing system allows you to keep that money coming in steadily, especially if you use our 5-Star Mailing System.** Again, the automated nature of our marketing system is very easy to understand. We put together a model called "$60,000 in 90 Days" because we wanted to helpfully and easily illustrate how powerful it is. Here's how "$60,000 In 90 Days" works: You use our automated system to bring in just four people in your first month. That's four people who made you $4,000, right? You make $1,000 on every sale we make for you. That's all you have to do. That's how our automated system gets started.

Those four people also get our automated system. **We want to teach them to do the same thing, so we show them how to use that automated system.** In Month Two, we're going to show them how to each get four sales. That's four people times four sales. Do the simple math here; that's 16 sales that they've made for you in Month Two. But *you* also continue using the system in Month Two to make four more sales, just like you did in Month One. That's $4,000 more for you. So in Month One, you made $4,000; and in Month Two, you directly made another $4,000 from four more sales. But those four people you brought in in Month One also made four sales for $16,000 in bonus commissions to you. So you add that $16,000 in Month Two to the $4,000 you personally made, and that's a total of $20,000 just in Month Two. But in Month Three, the whole thing happens again.

You keep using the system to bring in four personal sales. That's another $4,000 you made. But, now you have eight people working for you: the four from Month One and the four from Month Two. If each of those eight goes out and makes four sales, that's $32,000 — plus the $4,000 you brought in. That's $36,000 you've made for Month Three. Month two was $20,000. Month one was $4,000. **When you add all that up, that's a cool $60,000 you've made just in your first 90 days using our system.** *That's* the power of our automated system.

Now, again, that's just a mathematical progression. Nobody's really going to have four sales who all make four sales every month. One or two people might do nothing. Maybe someone will sell six and someone else ten. But it could easily average out to four sales each. **The point is, you always get $1,000 for every sale you make or that we make for you. And you also get $1,000 every time we help one of your team members make a sale.** That mathematical example shows the power of our automated system because — again, as an example — if you bring in four people who each do the same, by Month Three you'll be pulling $36,000 in that month. And that can continue to grow, again, as more people join your team and both you and they continue to use the system. Because you continue to get a thousand dollars every sale that we help those people make... that can continue to grow! If after 90 days, you decide to stop, you might have 12 people in your team — and you'll still get $1,000 for every automated sale those 12 people make. So literally, you could work the system so that, after a few months, you could sit back, do nothing, and continue getting bonus checks for all the sales we made for all those people.

Again, the math will never work out *exactly* like that example. But that shows you how the system works. **And that shows you why our automated system is so powerful,** and why we're so excited about putting it in place for you.

Our 5-Star Mailing System is just a way to help advertise the free book that leads the whole thing off. Let's say you go out there, and you're mailing 500, 1,000, 2,000 postcards a month, all offering that free book. People receiving those cards will go to your website, they'll pay $5 to get the free book, and then we'll promote the opportunity to them. For every one of the people who goes ahead and purchases a seminar ticket, a check for $1,000 shows up in your mailbox a week later. It doesn't get any easier than that, does it?

We called this opportunity "CLUB-20 International" because if you use our automated system to attract four distributors that we place into your team who also then turn around and use it to do the same thing, **on average, you'll have 20 distributors total.** If all of those people just made one sale every month, you'd get $20,000 a month. If they made one sale every two months, you'd get $10,000. The "International" part comes from our intention of taking this thing international — **so you can tap into a truly global market.**

CHAPTER THREE:

The Five Magic Keys to Wealth

Let's move on to our next set of criteria: the Five Magic Keys to Wealth, which every opportunity must have in order to potentially bring in millions of dollars. This is another formula that we've used again and again. Most of the Keys are related to what I've already talked about, though once again, there are some unique things to cover here.

I'm going to cover the first two Keys as if they're one, because they're so tightly connected. The <u>FIRST</u> <u>MAGIC</u> <u>KEY</u> to wealth is this: **There has to be an established and growing market for the business.** The <u>SECOND</u> <u>MAGIC</u> <u>KEY</u> is: **It must be something that's new or different that sets you apart from the competitors.**

Clearly, there's a fine line that you have to walk between those two things. I call it "the razor's edge." **On one hand, it's got to be part of something established, something steady, something ongoing right now. And on the other hand, it's got to be something new, something different.** If it's too new, then it's unproven and risky. If it's too established, then it's boring and more of a commodity, and it doesn't really get people excited. So clearly, the line you've got to walk is very fine, but nonetheless, you have to be able to walk that line to survive. It's kind of like a circus tightrope act!

Let's look a little closer at <u>THE</u> <u>FIRST</u> <u>KEY</u>. You want something that's proven; you don't want to be pioneering a new idea. We've seen entrepreneurs who try to go create or promote something brand new, and it rarely works out. There are too many variables, too many things that are out of your control. You're entering into a marketplace where you have to educate people on why there's a need or even a want for such a product or service. Well, that's too risky. **That's why you want to get into a marketplace that's already established, where there's a strong demand for the types of products or services you want to sell.** Then from that point, armed with that information, you set out to create or develop products that offer something new or different.

It's like building a better mousetrap. People already have mice and are already using mousetraps, so that's nothing new. But you can build a better one! You do something different that more effectively catches mice. **So basically, you start with something people already know about** — in other words, they're already educated on why this is something they want or need — **and you're coming at them with a new product, a new service, something that builds upon something they already understand and that you don't have to educate them about.** You're combining those two in a delicate balance.

One of the reasons I love the opportunity market is because it's a huge, established market that's growing fast. And yet, there's always something new coming into that market! Our challenge as marketers is to find that one aspect of our company and an offer that sets us apart and gets people excited. When it comes to the opportunity market, there's been a whole lot of water under the bridge; there's been a whole lot of stuff that's come before us; and there will be much, much more arriving in the future, because there's a demand. **People want what we have to offer.** It's very exciting to me to know that I'm engaged in a marketplace that's filled with people who are hungry for what I offer!

With CLUB-20 International, our marketplace is

twofold. One market represents the 30-50 million small business owners in America who are looking for a way to make more money. Those business owners are faced with all kinds of problems. For example, technology that's actually helped small-business people has also become a hindrance to them. That technology has empowered the average individual, so it's easier for people to get into business, which has increased the competition. There's a flood of new businesses aided by this technology, and it's making it extremely difficult for existing small business owners. That's why they're looking for a way to make more money, and that's why this is one of the two growing markets that CLUB-20 International serves. We do that through our coaching programs, through our twice-yearly seminars, and through products and services that are designed to help small business people gain that advantage over their competition so they can compete successfully — and make more money.

The second market includes those who either have home businesses now or are thinking about starting a business. We see this as a huge opportunity for us in the future. As Ralph Waldo Emerson said back in the 1850s, "America is another name for opportunity." **People are looking for a way to make more money and be independent, and we're here to help them.**

Those two markets are huge, well-established, and growing. There's lots of demand there, and we fill that demand with innovative proprietary products and services that are also highly profitable, with our automated marketing system doing all the selling. **The fact that they are established *and* growing markets is important, because if the marketplace is stagnant, it's useless to us.** Now, you could have a well-established market, like building fire hydrants, that's pretty stagnant. People have been building fire hydrants for decades, but the market isn't exactly growing. Maybe in some cities they're putting in more fire hydrants here and there, but there's no way that fire hydrant manufacturing is an exciting, growing business.

It's critical to have a marketplace that's growing if you want to maximize your chance of success. **The markets we're tapping here are ideal, especially as the Baby Boomers get older and move toward retirement age.** It's kind of an oxymoron. You might not think that as more people retire, more businesses would be started. But those retired Baby Boomers are going to be looking for something to do with themselves. Many of them will start their own home-based businesses — and they're all going to need marketing help and support. Some of them won't seek it, but they all need it! That's where companies like ours come in. Not only that, but all of the industries that serve the aged are going to have to expand as those 73 million Baby Boomers retire.

So these markets are well-established, and plenty of people are making money in both, which are factors we look for in any wealth-making opportunity. But we're also looking for that SECOND MAGIC KEY: **the opportunity has to be new and exciting.** Again, that may seem mutually exclusive with the first Magic Key, but that's not necessarily the case. They don't have to cancel each other out if you're careful. I think CLUB-20 International is a great example. We're brand new. As I write, we're still in pre-launch. And yet, the parent company standing behind it was established in September 1988, so you've got the proven track record stretching back 20+ years. We've built a better mousetrap, a reason to want to do business with us. We've got a new compensation plan, a new way of paying people lots of money upfront in the fastest possible time. Our "$60,000 in 90 days" deal is unique, something that people can understand quickly and want to be a part of. Who doesn't want to make $60,000 in the next 90 days? **People can easily understand that this is something *definitely* different from most MLM**

companies, which aren't easy to understand and are mostly "me too" organizations anyway.

Let's move on to the THIRD MAGIC KEY to Wealth: **You must have a strong answer for the skeptical people in your marketplace.**

Now, you might think, "Well, why would people be skeptical?" Well, they just are. It doesn't matter how sincere you are; you may be the most honest person on the planet, and your advertisement can tell them exactly how it is with no gray areas. You may be completely on the up and up (and we'd expect you to be), but that doesn't mean your prospects know that. And it doesn't mean that they trust you. **People are inherently skeptical,** and they should be. We always want to find out, "What's in it for you? Why are you making me this offer? What are you saying here? What does this mean?" We want to question everything, especially in this era of saturation media. As a marketer, you have to understand that from the beginning, so that when you're looking for opportunities, **you know to look for one that easily answers people's concerns.** Don't be afraid to bring that up during your due diligence, because having answers for people's skepticism is a valuable marketing tool. You have to be able to say something like, "I know you're probably skeptical, and this sounds too good to be true. But here's why it's not."

If you address that, then people won't feel like you're hiding behind something. They're going to be more open and receptive to your message. **So address their skepticism, and then have an answer for it.** It's always good to understand what people are going to be skeptical about. **It's always good to know their objections.** Why would people think that they shouldn't do business with you? Regardless of the opportunity you get involved with, or the product or service you're selling, think those things through. Write out a list of the top five objections people might have when they see your offer. What are the reasons they might say no?

You have to face the fact that more people don't buy than do; it doesn't matter what your product is. So why do people *not* buy? Answer those objections and think about why people are going to be skeptical. **You always have to assume that people don't believe you and they don't trust you;** you're sticking your head in the sand if you believe otherwise. What about your offer will make people wonder about it? What would make people wonder whether it's legitimate or not? **Address their skepticism, their concerns, and their doubts in your sales copy.** By doing that, you bring it right out in the open, provide the answers, and move people toward the sale.

Some entrepreneurs are blinded to their prospects' skepticism for a simple human reason: they naturally assume that because they're absolutely in love with what they're selling or promoting, everyone else will be too. Nothing could be further from the truth. **Now, you have to really believe in your product or service in order to maximize sales, but you can't blind yourself to problems or objections either.** People who do just don't want to get honest with themselves about the level of skepticism out there, and yet, we're living in the most skeptical time in history. I honestly believe that, and I think I have good reason. In the past, people had more respect for authority figures than they have today. Now almost everyone is suspect, from the President to the Pope. Everybody is doubtful, and they're not afraid to voice that skepticism like they used to be.

Sure, there's a lot of fraud out there. There's no question about it. But there's also a lot of media attention that amplifies every bad story. You have a situation where something bad happens in one part of the world and within minutes the whole world knows about it on their screen. **So people just don't trust anymore.** They don't trust their religious leaders, politicians — and they certainly don't trust salespeople. Everybody is suspect nowadays, and everybody is careful. Everybody is cautious. We're all trying to protect ourselves. And in some ways, we're foolish if we don't.

So when people are skeptical, you've got to have an answer for them. **When you proactively address any objections your prospects might have, you're achieving a positive result with a negative premise.** That's become one of the more effective ways of overcoming skepticism today. You can also beat people over the head with all the logical arguments of why they need to believe you. One of the best ways to do that is with income-specific verifiable testimonials that you can build into your sales material. **Look for opportunities that have those testimonials, because they go a long way toward overcoming skepticism.** You're not just making up a testimonial, saying, "This is J. K. from Texas. He made $100,000 in five minutes!" You've got to have something real and verifiable. Here's what we're doing right now for CLUB-20: we're setting up a testimonial hotline where people from all over can record their own audio testimonials in their own voices, accents and all. They're saying things like, "This is Carl Perkins down here in Birmingham, Alabama, and I just wanted to let you know..." You hear from Carl, and it's real!

It's okay to tell people what kind of testimonials you're looking for; in fact, that's what we're doing with our hotline. We're not saying, "Hey, here's what we'd like you to say: "T. J. Rohleder is the greatest person on Earth." What we're saying is, **"We'd like you to tell us how happy you are with our system. Please tell us how much money you've made; be specific."** A testimonial wouldn't be as good if it said, "I love this program. I made thousands of dollars!" A better testimonial would be, "I got started, and within my first six weeks I made $12,542.65." That's a dollar-specific testimonial: "Here's how much money I made, and here's how fast I made it."

A testimonial can also be more generic. It can say, "Hey, I bought this package, and I was skeptical, but when I opened it, it was everything I thought it would be and more. I'm so happy and I'm excited to get started!" **Happy, feel-good testimonials are valuable, too.** You want to get specific testimonials from people, who are talking about their happiness with doing business with the company, or how much money they've made using the system.

I've actually written sales letters based upon starting with all the objections, all the reasons under the sun that I can think of why somebody wouldn't buy — and then just seeing how I can shoot down or address each objection. Until that list was finished, I didn't feel like my selling job was complete. And ideally, in good sales material, for every objection you might have, you'll see a testimonial from someone other than the promoter that addresses your specific objection. If you think an opportunity might be a little inconvenient, ideally there's going to be a testimonial somewhere in that sales material that says, "I thought this was going to be inconvenient, but I got in and I discovered this is more convenient than anything else."

If there's one quality that all great salespeople have, it's that they love objections. They want objections! And one of the reasons they want objections is because the prospect who has no objections is usually not a *good* prospect. They're not engaged at all. **The most serious buyers out there have *lots* of objections.** They've got lots of questions they want answered, so you've got to have those answers.

Remember, people just don't believe anything anymore. They don't trust anything. **And what we're doing to counter that is offering this big beautiful book that's the foundation of our automated marketing system.** It's 472 pages long, and it took a lot of work to put this book together. Even if people get it and don't read it, it's designed to establish credibility. If you haven't seen it yet, it's a bit of an odd book, because it's actually two books in one; the first consists of all the pages on the left side, the other all the pages on the right. Again, it's designed for skeptics. **It helps to establish our credibility, to prove that we are experts at what we do.** It's also free; they can get it for only $5 shipping and handling, so it lowers that barrier of entry. If somebody is skeptical, they're not going to want to pony-up a lot of money, until and unless, they know that you're somebody they can count on, that you have credibility, that you're trustworthy, and they know something about you. The book is designed to do a lot of that.

Again, people generally have several objections. They want to know, "What's in it for you? Why would you share your greatest wealth-making idea with me? If it's so good, why are you giving it to me?" We tell them, **"Hey, we make $1,000 on our main product every time we help *you* make $1,000. That's why we're willing to give you the system. That's why we're willing to work with you and do everything for you."** Now that's gross income, not net income, but still, it gives us every incentive to help people make money.

People also want to know why and how you're able to do this. If you make an offer that seems unreasonable, how are you able to do that? You have to answer that. Don't be afraid to bring it up. "I know you're skeptical. Here's why you shouldn't be…" If you don't address it, they're already thinking it, and you can't keep them from thinking it; all you can do is your best to help overcome it.

The FOURTH KEY TO WEALTH: **You must build residual income into your entire business plan.**

Let me use an example I learned from my friend Chris Hollinger. When he was fresh out of college, the father of one of his basketball teammates was a very successful life insurance salesman. The man knew that that was what his job was: to sell life insurance. That's what put bread on the table. He also knew, that every single year he was going to be paid at least $150,000 before he sold a thing — because he'd been in the business for a number of years and had a lot of residuals built up. When Chris heard that, his eyes lit up. Wow, $150,000 a year? He was like, "Yeah, I want to do this!"

So for a while, Chris sold life insurance. He says it was fun; he learned a lot. But when you get right down to it, life insurance selling isn't much different than all those Network Marketing companies out there. What do they have you do? They have you sit down and make a list of everyone you can sell a life insurance policy to, which is just what they do with Network Marketing. Insurance has residuals. And guess what? From his time as a life insurance salesman, Chris still gets little checks that show up at his mother's house, because that was his address at the time. He'll go visit his Mom and there'll be a stack of checks there. They're never for much money, so eventually, he just told his Mom, "From now on, just put my signature on them and put them in your bank account. I don't even want to see them."

Residual income like that (but ideally in larger amounts, of course) should be a part of your marketing business, because it helps level out some of the ups and downs that you'll face. It makes things easier, because you've got built-in income you can count on. Now, Chris also used to be a schoolteacher, and one of the things that he and his wife liked about that was that there was a set amount of money coming in every single month that they could depend on, regardless of their actions. Like any marketing business, their current promotional-based income revolves around them keeping those plates spinning.

Understandably, **the potential for residual income is something that attracts a lot of people to home-based business opportunities, and it's definitely something that you really want to take a close look at.** Does that residual income come from thousands of people's actions, or can you get enough of a residual income without having to look at the compensation plan and say, "Okay, I really won't have a residual income until there's 20,000 people below me?" Or, "Can my efforts and the efforts of a good marketing system consistently put money in my pocket month after month?" If the answer to that question is "Yes!", then the opportunity truly offers a residual income you can depend on for at least a while.

Residual income is freedom; it's a liberating experience. Some business opportunities provide it and some don't. **CLUB-20 does.** Now, let's just take a look at our core products. We do have coaching programs that have monthly fees you can earn residual income on, but as I've mentioned before, our main product is our three-day Wealth Explosion Seminar, which earns you $1,000 on every sale we make for you and $1,000 for every sale we make for the people who join your team. So every time we work with the clients that you bring into the system — every time we help them make a sale — you automatically earn a residual income. **Those commissions are paid weekly;** if you go out this week and you make a sale, a check arrives next week. The same thing happens for all the people we put into your team. If we've got people on your team who are out there earning money and making sales, those bonuses are going to be sent to you like clockwork on a weekly basis. Every week, we have someone tally up all the commissions that were earned, and we immediately send them out. That way you can earn residual income that's not just paid monthly, but actually *weekly.*

And last, but not least: the FIFTH MAGIC KEY to Wealth. **The opportunity has to have a slack adjuster.**

A slack adjustor is a high-ticket item that pays you huge profits. Because the perceived value of the products and services is so high, and because through the miracle of technology the delivery cost can be low, that leaves a lot of leftover money to pay yourself. **This is really important, because if your business is missing a slack adjustor, you're leaving money on the table.** All marketers have a segment of their customer base that wants to spend more money with them. But if you don't make them a big-ticket offer, they're not going to be spending that money with you.

That's a big mistake, which is why it's so important to have a slack adjustor here. Until you come along and you make one of these leads or customers an offer at a higher price, you're not going to get that amount. If you only go around saying, "Can I have a hundred bucks? Can I have a hundred bucks?" that's all you're going to get. But if you stop and say, "Hey, does anybody want to give me $3,000, or $5,000, or $10,000?" there will be a fraction of people in that marketplace who *will* want to give you that much money... and a smaller number who will want to give you even more! **Just having one slack adjustor can dramatically shift the numbers and make things wildly profitable.** So maybe you made a bunch of small sales to acquire customers; well, you only need to make a few big slack adjuster sales to really start feeling the profit.

I can't overstate the importance of a slack adjustor in any business opportunity. Everything costs more than you think it will, and all the little things really do add up. My mentor Russ von Hoelscher tells this great story about how he grew up in Minnesota, and there's this place in the northern part of the state where there's a stream that's considered the birthplace of the Mississippi River. Russ says that you can actually step across it — it's a very *small* stream. But if you think about it, by the time it drains into the sea, that mighty river is composed of a bunch

CHAPTER THREE: The Five Magic Keys To Wealth

of other streams that came together across thousands of miles. **Your daily bills and expenses can add up like that, too. It's the slack adjustor that helps pay those bills,** so getting those nice checks coming in regularly is something we look for in every opportunity.

Now, I have friends (who will remain unnamed) who have a hard time selling things that are expensive. In fact, it's almost impossible for them to do it. It's because they just can't get their heads around the idea of the slack adjustor. It's just fear; that's all it is. One of these good friends is somebody that I care a lot about, and I hate to see him struggling. I've always wondered why he can't comprehend this idea of selling things for more money. And then, recently, I listened to a program where the speaker said, "If you're the kind of person who is extremely frugal about every little purchase that you make, and you're counting the pennies on every little thing... then you're never, ever, going to be able to sell anything expensive." And it finally made sense to me. I've wondered for years why an otherwise brilliant marketer could struggle so much with selling things for high prices. I understand it now! I realized, that's my friend! He's that way with money. Every little thing he buys, I don't care what it is, he's careful with. He knows the price of everything, and he's always counting his pennies. No wonder he can't sell high-ticket items! *He thinks that everybody is like that.* He automatically assumes that because he's like that, everybody else is too. But there are a lot of people like me, who don't look at or care about prices. I just buy what I want! I have no problem with selling things for more money.

With CLUB-20 International, our flagship product is our $3,000 seminar. The $1,000 commission you get for that is a pretty darn good slack adjuster. **Obviously, the term "slack adjustor" means taking up the slack in your cash flow.** Advertising is expensive, and a slack adjustor can help offset the costs of acquiring a new customer. It can help put you in maximum profits in the fastest time. When you give away our free book, you obviously have to spend money to advertise that book. Now, there are free things you can do — free classified ads, free publicity — but generally those are more indirect and don't really bring you very good results. **So we recommend that you actually spend money to target and advertise.** That's obviously an expense; giving away a free book doesn't make you any money, right? You need a big-ticket backend item like our Wealth Explosion Seminar, which pays you $1,000 every time someone says yes. So you bring in a bunch of leads who want the free book. We work with those leads, a percentage of those leads purchase our seminar, and you get paid your $1,000 on each.

But, we have coaching programs available, and **those are even *better* slack adjusters.** Anybody who signs up for our free book is informed about our coaching programs. We have a variety of them, all the way up to one that costs almost $18,000 a year. Obviously it's a high-level program, not suitable for that many people. But you get paid a substantial commission on it; so there are additional opportunities there to adjust the slack.

Now, clearly, not everybody is going to qualify for that program. We actually interview people for that package and don't accept everybody. In fact, we've turned away more people than we've accepted into the Platinum Plus coaching program. But, we also have a $5,000 coaching program, a $1,250 coaching program, and a $500 coaching program. **Those additional products and services are made available to your clients to help adjust that slack and help you make more money.** And again, we take care of all that for you! If our client service representatives are on the phone talking to somebody, and they find out this person is really looking for some advanced marketing help, we can tell them, "Hey, we have a coaching program available. Here are the main benefits. Would you like to get started on that today?" and they can sign them up. That's something that automatically happens, and a check would be sent out to you because they were *your* client.

I think that's pretty exciting! It goes back to automatic cash, which is the FOURTH MAGIC KEY to Wealth. All of our stuff sells for big-ticket prices, and we know it sells well. In fact, as I've said, we've been promoting CLUB-20 International for only a few months, yet as of this writing, we are almost already SOLD OUT and taking advance orders for our next Wealth Explosion Seminar. Talk about your wealth explosion!

Chapter Four:

The 27 Problems

In this chapter, I'll discuss the 27 problems that our 20+ years of research has demonstrated are inherent in most business opportunities and **the way that CLUB-20 International addresses those.** Some of these problems are closely related to each other, and some will echo some of the items from the previous chapters. However, I do think it's important to re-emphasize all of these items.

The <u>FIRST</u> <u>PROBLEM</u> is this: **Most new opportunities are new and unproven.**

When you look at such opportunities, it just looks like somebody came up with a good idea for making money, wrote up a report or published a book about the opportunity, and now they want to sell it to you. That's how they make their money, in the selling of the idea. **They have no vested interest in your success.** Once they sell you the program, they're outta there. A lot of these ideas sound great. You get all excited about them... **and then you find there's no track record.** If the idea itself is unproven, then you're going to be losing your money.

So with every opportunity, you should always ask yourself: "Who are the people behind it? Do they make a majority of their profits from a percentage of the money that they help you make? What's their record of past performance?" Even if they're good, honest people — as I believe most are — how can they really help you if they've never made substantial amounts of money themselves? It's like reading a diet book — and then finding out the author is fat.

So I would be very, very careful about the people behind the opportunity. I would look for what they've done before. If the opportunity is brand new, that's fine if the people behind it **a)** have a proven track record of past performance and **b)** make the majority of their profits from helping their clients. How long have they been in business? Where do they come from? What's their background? Is there anything that would give you reason to believe that they'll lead you where you want to go? The worst thing you can do is follow somebody who's leading you in the wrong direction! It would be better to stand still. So when you're evaluating opportunities, figure out where they're going and whether they can take you along. Are they following the same path you're on?

There's a cliché that we've all heard: that the pioneers are the ones who get scalped. That's also true in business. Sometimes you can make a lot of money by being first, but sometimes it's the worst possible thing you can do. Don't cast yourself as a pioneer with a new opportunity that's totally unproven. **If the people behind it have never done anything of any substantial nature, that's reason enough to stay away from them.** You also want to look at why it's unproven; just because something is new doesn't necessarily mean it's bad. But you've got to find something there that gives you a reason to hope and a reason to believe in that opportunity before latching on to it.

Although CLUB-20 International is brand new, our company is not. **We've been around for a couple decades now.** If you join CLUB-20, you'll be making money with the same types of products and services that we've sold tens of millions of dollars worth ourselves. We have a vested interest in helping you. **So while it's new, it's definitely not unproven in any way, shape, or form.** The suppliers that we're hooking you up with via our 5-Star Mailing System have been companies that we've used since the early to mid-1990s. We've done millions of dollars worth of business with these suppliers; that's something you don't get very often. Usually, when you get involved in an opportunity where you're riding a new wave, you find you're also riding a company that's only been in existence since last Tuesday, and the guy running it is some nerd with a great looking website who's sitting in a little office in a dingy, dank basement.

Well, as I've already mentioned, **we're for real.** We started our business in 1988, and we've had our own building since 1991. We've had the same phone number for all those years. We're accessible. You can just show up one day during the week, even though it's not real comfortable for us, because we like to roll out the red carpet. We like to know when people are coming to visit us, but you *can* just show up and we'll find some staff who can sit down and talk to you. So we're here. **We're a real company that's backed by 20 years of business, and you just don't get that with very many opportunities.** Our very first seminar was September 22, 1990. I remember that date well, because I was scared to death. It was the most frightening day of my life!

Since then, we've had hundreds of events like the one this opportunity sells, so it's not like we're unproven event promoters. The fact that we've now wrapped an opportunity around one of those events is nothing that you should worry about, even though it's a brand new opportunity. Same thing with our coaching programs; we've been offering coaching for all those years as well. So again, while we have a brand new opportunity, **it's based on our company's successful track record of helping people since way back in 1988.** You've got something that's a lot of the old and a little of the new mixed together.

The SECOND BIG PROBLEM is, **Most of the moneymaking methods are the same boring plans and**

programs that will never make you rich.

They're not going to make you rich for a number of reasons, and one of those is just because they're boring. The problem with most opportunities is that they sell what I consider "me too" products and services. Everybody sells them. They've been around for a long time. Everything they give you is old news; there's nothing new and exciting about them. **They're selling the same thing, using the same methods.** You've heard it before, even if it's "new"—because you've been exposed to similar things from other companies. They use the same tired, worn-out sales method. The terminology they use is the same. It's all boring.

When you're evaluating an opportunity, **you need to look for something that's new and exciting.** So ask yourself, is there something that would give you a reason to be excited about offering this or telling people about it? Are you concerned that when you talk to people, they're going to already know about it? Have they heard it before? Does it sound similar? If there's nothing new and exciting about it, if there's nothing that gives you a reason to think that it's not like everything else, stay away from it. **So make sure the product is fresh, and that it rides a trend that has a lot of potential.** We've done this for years. Back in the early 1990s, when computer bulletin boards were new, we were showing people how to make money on them. In the mid-1990s, when the Internet was just taking off, we showed people how to profit on that. We did it with domain names in the late 1990s, before the dot-com crash, when people were rabidly buying Internet property. Later, we taught people how to make money on eBay.

So we've always been at the cutting-edge of things that were new, things that were not what you would consider "me too" products. **That's the trick: to offer things that are new and exciting, that don't sound tired and worn out.** Again, most Network Marketing is pretty much the same. The marketing approach is simple, as I've pointed out: you start out trying to sell to people you know. The only things that make that industry vibrant are revolutionary products that people can get excited about. It ends up being the same type of marketing, even when used for new, exciting products.

Chris Hollinger recently recounted a conversation he had with one of the big guys in a Network Marketing company he was participating in. The guy called Chris and wanted to talk about his approach to marketing and the mechanisms and strategies he used. He said, "Chris, if full-page ads and direct mail worked, don't you think we'd be doing it?" Chris said, "Well, it's working for me — or you wouldn't be talking to me right now." The reason he called Chris was because Chris was making a lot of sales — and he was complaining about the way Chris was making those sales, which is pretty ironic! **The point is, there's money to be made even with some tired, old programs if your marketing is fresh.** One of the reasons the programs stop being effective in the first place is that marketers just churn out the same old marketing.

Now, I pointed out in the previous section that your product and service can't be too new or revolutionary, because that means it's unproven. But at the same time, you can't just spout and sell the same old boring stuff — so there's a delicate line here. There's a Biblical passage from the book of Ecclesiastes that points out, "There's nothing new under the sun." That was written 600 years before Christ. While it's not entirely true (at least, not in these days of high technology), I think you get the point.

At some level, a lot of stuff that's "new" really isn't all that new. Sometimes it's something old that someone's put a new veneer on or given a new twist to. That's a good thing: there's got to be something to captivate people. If the opportunity itself doesn't make you excited, then it's probably not such a great opportunity. If you're not even excited, how are other people going to get excited? Again, it's a delicate balancing act. If it's too new, then it's unproven. But if it's too old, then it's boring. **So again, you're looking for a proven track record of past performance, where the people behind it have a vested interest in your success.** I think that's more important than anything else.

Twice, I was a member of a big MLM company out of Michigan, which will remain nameless. Once I joined because my Dad got me to; the other time one of my co-workers got me to join. You know, that company is just boring! It's a boring, old company. Now, I think it's a *good* company. You might still be able to get rich with that opportunity... but it's going to be an uphill battle all the way. It's the same with most MLM companies. People are attracted to something that's new, different, and exciting, so you have to give them that — while providing something stable they can count on. That's what CLUB-20 International provides you through M.O.R.E., Inc.

We're different and unique because we've been around so long and have a track record of success. **We have an infrastructure (unlike most of these opportunities), and we provide all the help you need.** And again, our products and services are unique. A lot of these guys are selling the same old products. The way it usually works is, when one company launches a product that's successful, all of a sudden there are 20 different companies copying it — all with the same compensation plan, selling the same product using the exact same pay structures. It's all the same.

We built this company based on proprietary products. **We're the only ones putting on Wealth Explosion Seminars;** you're not going to get that anywhere else. **No one else can offer the coaching we offer you, either.** So this is a very unique opportunity backed by unique products and services. But as I've pointed out, we also feel **we have the best compensation plans that pay people the biggest profits in the fastest time — and that separates us from the pack as well.**

PROBLEM NUMBER THREE: **Most moneymaking programs only make the promoters rich.**

If you're considering an opportunity, **take a really good look at the compensation plan in comparison to the amount of money you'd spend to get into an opportunity.** Where is the money going? If their compensation plan is very weak on the front-end and on the back-end, then the money's going mostly to those people promoting the opportunity. Another clue is if the big money doesn't even kick in unless you've got a humongous downline; that's another indication that they don't really intend to pay out much in commissions.

A lot of them are just there to take advantage of you; they perceive you as an "easy mark." My colleagues and I have attended some big Network Marketing events where the language batted around by the owners was just appalling, where maybe their guard was down and their true colors were shining through. Now, I'm not saying they're all like that... but some are. For those people, their only motive is to make money at your expense, not by helping you. We're not going to name names for legal reasons, but here's a good example: recently there was a program that Chris Hollinger was very much involved in — until he went to one of their conventions in Dallas. All of a sudden he went from being very excited to being very cold. He got involved because a friend was involved in it, and he liked the technology. But once Chris had the opportunity to touch base with some of the people behind the thing, he just got a feeling about it... and after a while he thought it wisest to get out before he sunk even more money into promoting it for his business.

So don't just dive in. **Spend some time with the compensation plan, and if you're not getting a high front-end and a nice residual, then stay away from it** — because the money is going somewhere, and it's not going to you. So many programs out there should be sold in the fiction section of the bookstore. Somebody comes up with a great idea, it sounds good, they put a program together, and it's never been tested... it's never been proven... it doesn't work... and nobody ever makes any money. Worse, they're out there stabbing you in the back, with no vested interest in helping you. So just be careful!

Even if they do intend to help you at first, after a time they might just stop caring, because they're not incentivized by your success. If you're in their downline and they're only getting a few cents when you sell something, why should they care? No matter how good a person is, he or she is motivated by self-interest to some degree. We all are; it's within our nature. Maybe there's a person on this Earth who's not motivated by self-interest, but I don't know of any.

So you've got to find companies that have a vested interest in helping you succeed. According to the U. S. Department of Commerce, over 95% of small businesses started today will be gone five years from now. Those are terrible statistics. What's also true, according to that same U. S. Department of Commerce, is that 80-85% of all franchises that start today will still be going strong five years from now. The only real difference between a franchise and a traditional business is that with a franchise, you've got the support, help, and guidance of a company that's incentivized to keep doing whatever they can to help you. *That's* what you have with CLUB-20 International.

The question that you need to ask here is: "What's in it for me? What's in it for the person who's putting the opportunity together? Is there an incentive for them to help me? What do I get in return for the money I spend? Is there a way for them to help me and help themselves at the same time?" With a lot of opportunities, there's no real substance behind the offer. You spend your money and you get nothing in return. **If there's no way for them to be incentivized when they help you, they're probably not going to be there when you need them.** If you can't find that connection, you might want to look elsewhere — especially if they say something all warm and fuzzy like, "Hey, we really just like to help people!" Maybe it's true, but I'd be a little bit leery. You should either turn around and walk out, or do a little more due diligence before you get involved with them.

PROBLEM NUMBER FOUR: **Many of the most exciting ways to make money are either illegal or immoral.**

Why is that? **Because it's what the marketplace wants.** Now, one of the basic tenets of marketing is to give the market what it wants to buy — **but you have to be able to do it legally and morally.** Not just because you're a good person, though that should be enough, but because you want to keep making money from the opportunity for a long time. You don't want it shut down by the government before you can make the maximum possible profit, and you certainly don't want to go to jail for it. So before entering into any business opportunity, compare it against your ethical framework, where you've laid the things you're willing to do for money, and the things you'll *never* do for money. That way, when you're looking at a business opportunity you can say, "You know what? I'm not comfortable with that." Or, "I'm comfortable with that." **And, not everything that's legal may be morally acceptable to you.** For example, you may not want to be involved with anything dealing with pornography, alcohol, tobacco, or whatever. That's up to you.

The point is, if we wanted to make money irrespective of laws and morals, we could just start dealing drugs. We could start selling crack on the street corner, because ya know, the stuff really sells itself. You just do a free trial so people become addicts, and they'll never stop buying: they'll lie, cheat, steal, and kill just to get enough money to consume more. You can quickly make a ton of money that way, sure — but by no stretch of the imagination could it be considered legal or moral.

By knowing that the people at the top are ethical and they're doing things legally, you can have faith in the opportunity and feel good about getting involved in it. So ask yourself, has the company been around for a long time? Who are the leadership? Can you meet them? Can you trust them? If you can't get ahold of customer support, or they're hiding behind an Internet website and don't seem like real, three-dimensional human beings, those should be red flags for you. I'd be very reluctant to join a business opportunity if you can't actually meet the person in charge or talk to customer support.

So when you get into a business opportunity, you want to make sure not only that you have the potential to make lots of money — you want to be able to look at yourself in the mirror at the end of the day. **You want to be proud of what you've done.** You want to be able to honestly tell yourself that you've helped people, that you've served people, so you can feel good telling your friends and family, "Sure, now I have a lot of money, and here's how I made that money." Because otherwise, we could all rob liquor stores or start adult websites. Now, that last one may be legal, but it's just beyond the limits of morality for me. **Keeping your morality firmly in place will prevent you from making mistakes.**

Incidentally, the best time to think about this is right now, when there's not an offer in front of you, when you're in a detached, neutral state, so you can reason and logic without distraction. Sometimes, when you see a hot offer, if you don't have your ethics codified and you don't know what the business opportunity really entails, it's easy to be emotionally swayed —

enough that you actually end up joining an opportunity that involves something you don't feel comfortable doing.

And again, **you have to do your due diligence and check out the program in detail** — because often the hottest ones, the ones that seem too good to be true, really *are* too good to be true. Eventually they get shut down by the government, leaving you high and dry. **First of all, there has to be a real product involved. Second, you can't be forced or urged to do anything illegal or of questionable morality.** So question things and be careful, because there are a lot of sharks lurking behind nice websites and attractive offers. We see that all the time in the business opportunity market.

You know, there was a time, years ago, when it really upset me to see some of these companies get shut down by the government. I got going on this big anti-government crusade, as if it were the government's fault for shutting them down. Well, it's 30 years later, and I'm 30 years smarter... and I've seen a lot of things happen. I've done my research. Have some good companies gotten shut down by the government? Yes. But most of the time, when a company gets shut down, it's for a reason. It's because they're shady and have been doing illegal things.

Even if what a company's selling isn't explicitly illegal or immoral, oftentimes they're still screwing you around, because there's no viable market for the products or services being sold, at least outside of the distributor base. That's one of the biggest problems these companies have. **Whatever they're offering, it's just a scheme to get people involved.** When you try to find out what the product is, they keep steering you back to the compensation plan. If that's the case, a red flag should go up! That would be a good sign that they might be doing something illegal or immoral. Now, maybe not; maybe they're just really proud of their compensation plan. But they should at least be able to tell you what the product is without you having to prod constantly.

And here's another thing you can watch out for: **if they don't tell you how much the product or service costs, you're being played.** You'll notice that we tell you that our Wealth Explosion Seminar costs $3,000. But you don't have to buy it; you can become a distributor and sell it for free. We charge a $97 annual distributor fee, and the first year is free. Some companies require you to buy the product to be a distributor; you have to pay to play. Well, that's also a sure sign that something's not right. That's illegal.

Now, **we do have a qualification process you have to go through;** I've explained that a bit. You bypass that by having your own seminar ticket, **so there's an incentive to make a purchase; but it's not required.** You could go out today, use our automated system, start selling seminar tickets, and qualify for those $1,000 commissions after your first four sales.

PROBLEM NUMBER FIVE: **So many opportunities are here today and gone tomorrow.**

A lot of opportunities are built on fads, but to really succeed, **you've got to look for long-term opportunities.** Find products and services in marketplaces that are big and growing; that's always the secret for long-term success. Is there a viable need for the product or service? And is it part of a growing trend? I would stay away from fads, and as I said in the previous section, I would stay away from opportunities, no matter how popular, where the product has no real market outside of the distributors that sell it.

Back to Network Marketing again. **Too often, you look at the products and services being sold, and they're not really economically viable.** So why are they selling them? Well, their marketing system needed a product, and this is what they have. Another thing that you can look out for is over-priced products and services. A bottle of juice that might sell for one price in a store sells for twice or three times that through a Network Marketing opportunity. Things like that don't always indicate that there's a problem, but there's always that possibility. Now, maybe that juice has a special ingredient in it that makes it expensive — so that's not to say that a can of apple juice should cost you the same price as a bottle of some juice from South America that contains a special ingredient that has some miracle benefit. But how likely is that?

Take a look at our opportunity, and **you'll find that our coaching programs and seminars are priced comparably to similar products and services offered by other companies.** That's something you should do with any opportunity. Look at the price of what they're selling; does it seem to fit? If it's too expensive, it probably means the only people buying it are those who have to — because the company says that if you don't buy 15 jars of this and store it in your garage, you can't be an XYZ member, and you can't maximize the compensation plan. If the price is too high relative to the general marketplace of other similar products and services, that would be a red flag.

I think your most valuable asset is your time, because that's not replaceable. Unlike money, once you've spent an hour or a day on something, you can never get that time back; whereas if you lose a little bit of money, you can work a little and get it back. **So you want to invest your time in an opportunity that's going to be around for the long haul.** That's another reason it's very smart to do your due diligence up front.

One reason that so many business opportunities are here today, gone tomorrow ties in with the concept of technology lowering the barrier of entry, making it easier and easier for people to get started. Anybody can have a nice-looking website for a few hundred dollars now. In fact, you can basically put one together for free if you know a little about HTML. But who's behind those nice looking websites? They might be Charles

Manson-type people. I mean, think about the creepiest person you've ever seen in your life; *that* might be the person behind those websites. You just never know. It's easier today than ever before to build a website and hide behind it.

One thing you want to look out for is if the website doesn't have any contact information. Ask yourself, "Why?" If it doesn't list who owns the website or give you a phone number or tell you how to contact them, why? Now, I *will* say that in some cases they don't want you to contact them because they don't want you to bypass their sales process. Some websites have splash pages where they want you to give them your contact information, and they're afraid that if they tell you who they are you'll just Google them and bypass the splash page. **They want you to give them *your* contact information.** So not everybody who doesn't list their information is hiding something, but in general that's what you see with bad companies. That's something that you've got to look out for. These companies will often set up a website and run it for a while; then they'll bounce and they'll create another website. You can spend money with them, and then find that you have no way of contacting them after the sale. They never told you who they were, so there's no way to return the product. Even if there is, **look for companies that don't offer guarantees.** Those kinds of companies are usually here today and gone tomorrow. There are so many fly-by-night opportunities out there.

But CLUB-20 International is solidly backed by M.O.R.E., Inc. We've been around for a long time. We're proud of our staff. We've invested a ton of money in our infrastructure. We hire only the best people. **We offer the best guarantees,** because offering a guarantee is a great way to remove the skepticism and also show people, hey, we're here for the long haul! **You can come check it out, and there's no risk — no obligation.** Hey, if you don't like what you hear, if we're not able to help you, we don't want to keep your money. And even if you don't want to buy right away, we still encourage people to come visit us. It's not the easiest thing to come to Goessel, Kansas; we don't have a big airport or anything. But we're accessible. People *can* come visit us if they want. We love to give people tours of our shop. We're proud of what we do; we're proud of our infrastructure.

On to <u>PROBLEM</u> <u>NUMBER</u> <u>SIX</u>: **Most opportunities have no way to help you make huge amounts of money.**

Help? With a lot of opportunities, that's a four-letter word! They've never heard of help. **They don't want to help you.** They want you to do everything yourself. They want you to figure out everything on your own; they even want you to figure out how you're going to sell their product. They hope you'll talk to your friends, but they certainly won't offer to help you do that. They certainly don't have a sales staff that's willing and able to help you close your sales. They certainly don't have a way to help you make money with their system, because they don't even have a system! **Most opportunities can't help you make money at all, because they leave everything to you.** You've got to figure out how you're going to advertise; you've got to figure out how you're going to bring in money. How are you going to talk to people? What are you going to do? All the details are left to you. They may give you some basics, but that's it; beyond that there's no plan of action. There's no real vested interest on their part, so it's all just smoke and mirrors at best.

Some of these companies are run by people who are literally working by themselves, and they've got no infrastructure in place. One of the things we like to tell people is that we've got a staff. You want to talk about help? **Not only do we have customer support people to help you on the phone, we have a client/service representative team in place that actually helps you close sales so that you don't have to talk**

to people!

So you need to look at how an opportunity helps you. If there's no help, that's a red flag. Then look at the degree to which they're willing to help you, the effort they'll go to in order to help you make money. The more that they're in a position to make money by helping you, the more likely they *are* to help you. Again, **you want to stay away from people who don't earn a significant part of their profits from helping *you* make money.** So if you ask them, "What's in it for you?" and they can't give you a fast, straight, clear answer, then grab your wallet and back out the door.

PROBLEM NUMBER SEVEN: just like that song by the Steve Miller Band, **some opportunity promoters take your money and run.**

Unfortunately, one, or two, or a few bad apples can make the whole lot look bad. It's rare, but it does happen; in fact, there are grifters and con men out there who use that as their whole gig. They're simply on the other side of that illegal and immoral line. They've crossed over to the Dark Side, so to speak. And how do you spot them? Again, **it comes down to your due diligence.** And the Internet can help; you can't necessarily believe everything you read or hear on the Internet, but it can be a good tool to help investigate the true people behind opportunities. There are a lot of people out there that can make things sound really nice, and then the next thing you know they're off to Tahiti with your money.

Some of these people aren't using their real names, either. Here's an example: there's a fairly well known fellow in our market. I won't tell you his name, but he works out of Florida. He's nobody we're associated with, but he's somebody that we know of. I recently found out that the name he goes by isn't his real name. Maybe he changed it for marketing purposes, because his real name is kind of boring, and his fake name is much more exciting. I've met the man once in Chicago, about 10 years ago. Maybe he's got a legit reason for not using his own name... but you never know.

Scammers are always working up phony names and false drop addresses. It's easier for criminals to perform their crimes these days, too, by the way. So you've got to be careful. Anyone who looks suspicious is likely to cut and run on you. During your due diligence, if you see someone suspicious, **first try to find out if they're incorporated.** If their business name seems to be a corporation, you can double-check the public records and see if they're really a registered corporation in that state. For example, you can call the State of Kansas and find out that M.O.R.E, Inc. and CLUB-20 International are actually real companies. **Or if they give you a phone number, do a reverse phone number look-up online and see if the number actually matches their company.**

Even some of the bigger MLM companies are guilty of certain fly-by-night activities. In fact, some are infamous for hurting their best distributors. Some of these guys will spend years building a downline; they'll have hundreds or thousands of people in their organization, and then all of a sudden the company cuts them off. I've seen it happen many times over the last 30 years. The top distributors, the guys who are getting paid big bucks, are kicked out of the organization, and the company takes all their money. It's a dangerous world. You do have to be careful. **On the flip side, if you look for companies that pay the largest amount of commissions up-front, then you don't have to worry about situations like that.**

I'm sure that some of the people involved in these fly-by-night opportunities are good people... but most of them are the kind of slick promoter I've always been leery of. You know, if I wanted to, I could go buy a $5,000 suit. I don't know where I'd get it, but I'm sure there's somebody who would sell me one. I could have every hair of my head neatly in place and held back with hairspray. I could shave off my beard. Some people do all that, and they're just perfect — everything about them is perfect. Their teeth are so white it's blinding when they smile at you; every hair on their head is just where it should be; their shoes are shined; their actions are all well-coordinated.

My God, I don't trust those people!

But I'm sure some of them *are* trustworthy. It's just... who do you trust? Look, we are what we are. Some people like us; some people don't. That's always a chance you take whenever you're just yourself. **But again, our record stands for itself.** Our parent company has been in business since 1988, and we've got a real building. You can go on our parent company's website, www. moreincorporated.com, and see a picture of the hospital building where we maintain our offices. It's a huge building. It would be pretty difficult to uproot that and move it somewhere else!

PROBLEM NUMBER EIGHT: **Most opportunities force you to work long hours for little pay.**

As copywriters, we're taught to make irresistible offers. I wouldn't sell many products or services if I came out with a headline that said, "Hey, here's an opportunity that offers long hours, very little pay, and a low potential for profits. You might make nothing. You might lose lots of money!" Hah! That's a list I don't want! That's the most resistible kind of offer possible.

Unfortunately, most opportunities *do* **offer the low-pay, long-hours trap due to the way they're set up and structured.** They don't have automated marketing systems. They don't have the kind of training and the backing you'll see with a good opportunity. They're going to force you to work really long hours with little pay. And let me tell you something:

if I wanted to work really long hours with little pay, I'd go get a traditional job. But isn't that what we're all moving away from?

So what we're looking for is the exact opposite. Anytime there are long hours with little pay, it's not going to work on two different fronts — meaning that if you join an opportunity and put in those long hours for little pay, you end up with very little to show for it. **It's just really disheartening.** My friend and colleague Kent Sayre was recently telling me that when he first got started in MLM, he and a buddy were really hyped up about a MLM that had a horrible pay plan — they didn't know they were going to have to work long hours and get paid nothing. (They actually lost a little money in it.)

But because they knew nothing about marketing and had no training, they thought, "Hey, we've got a great idea. On January 1, everyone sets a New Year's resolution to make more money. Okay, great! So we want to hit these people right as they're making their New Year's resolutions." So they put up these little cards, "Make more money in 2004. Come to our free seminar." They rented a room, and put down a couple hundred bucks. They were going to have a rah-rah MLM seminar and enroll everybody; and they'd pick up five customers, who'd get five, and five, and five, and so on, and so forth... which never works.

And so they went downtown to the middle of Portland, Oregon, where 100,000 people were gathered to watch the ball drop and celebrate New Year's Eve — and they started passing out these cards to all these drunk revelers. Now, you've got to imagine this. Here are Kent and his buddy, and they're just totally clueless (his words, not mine). They're walking up to drunken revelers saying, "Hey, make more money in 2004!" And it was funny, because one of the drunks lit his little card on fire, and it was like a chain reaction — everybody else started taking their little cards and doing the same. This was their dream! They were excited! What they were supposed to do was go out and recruit like maniacs — and they *were* trying to do that. But everybody just started lighting their little cards on fire, and by then they had handed out over a thousand! And so later on, they held their seminar — and oops, nobody showed up, so they were out a few hundred dollars. And that was the end of it. I think that really epitomizes the concept of long work hours for little pay — in this case, no pay at all.

That's not very compelling. That's not very exciting. Even if anyone had showed up, they weren't going to enroll anyone anyway, because the system behind the opportunity wasn't easily duplicable. They didn't have anything. So any opportunity that's going to force you to work long hours with little pay won't work for you, and it won't work for anybody you're trying to recruit. Make sure to stay away from those. **What you need are those opportunities that provide big commissions on small numbers of sales and that let you earn the bulk of your income from other things besides your time.** That's the main thing. If it forces you to work a lot of hours, it's usually for low ticket items that you have to stay away from. There's just not enough money in it.

Now, contrast that with CLUB-20 International. **Just on our flagship product, you're getting paid $1,000 for every single sale.** That's a lot, and it's very different from most MLM companies, even the good ones, some of which we're involved with right now. I want to be completely upfront with you about that. The truth is, we're involved in some good MLM companies that offer low-ticket products and services, but only as part of our secondary business model. **Our primary business will always be focused on earning our money by helping people like you make money.** You've got to have something that brings in the big bucks. If you're going to be involved in low-ticket items, make sure it's secondary income, not primary income.

We've talked a little about how a lot of times when you get

into a business, you're just buying a job. For example: retail businesses where you have to go in early in the morning and stay late at night, and you're the main employee. You have other employees you have to worry about, and you've got to deal with a lot of headaches and hassles. If you're going to have that kind of thing, at least be selling a big-ticket item, so it's worth it in the end.

With CLUB-20 there are no long hours, and the pay is phenomenal. You can work very little and make big money. And again, our automated system puts it in place, so that you really can spend as little time on it as you want. I talked earlier about part-time, and this is what that is. **Part-time** could be as little as spending 10-15 minutes a day placing some classified ads on the Internet, or calling up some magazines and running classified ads. Or you could literally let our automated system do everything for you. You could fill out the 5-Star Mailing Systems form that lets us mail postcards for you. You could spend 10 minutes filling out that form once, send that in to us, and every month our suppliers would do all the work so that you wouldn't need to spend your time and energy doing it yourself. **So it can be hands-off completely,** and yet you can still make that $1,000 for every automated sale we make for you, and $1,000 for every automated sale we make for the people we place into your team. And that's just our flagship product; we offer other products and services that can make you even higher commissions than that.

PROBLEM NUMBER NINE: **Most opportunities offer products and services that nobody wants.**

MLM companies are infamous for this, where the only people who buy the products and services are the distributors themselves. There's no real market other than that. So the joke is, if you can't sell something any other way, you start a MLM company! But it's not a very funny joke, really. In the end, **you**

want products and services that excite people, things that people are gladly paying money for right now, things that are sold in non-MLM formats. But also realize, too, that sometimes those are faddish items, so you've got to be careful with that.

We're currently involved with a company that was selling their services long before they connected with a MLM system. They've been doing that for 40 years and have a huge track record of success, even from before they became a MLM company. In fact, I think they actually merged with an existing MLM company that then became their marketing branch. In any case, **that's what you need to look for: something with a proven track record outside of the realm of MLM.** Similarly, when you're talking about Network Marketing, if the product can't be sustained outside the Network Marketing infrastructure, there probably isn't a real marketplace for it anyway. Look for products that have potential even when there's no Multi-Level infrastructure in place to support them.

My best example of a product that can't make it on its own is specialty juice. There are so many MLM juice companies out there now! I swear, it's proof all over again that the market is saturated with copycats; there's very little creativity. Everybody's following the follower — or they're following one big leader, because in this case, it all started with a company in Salt Lake City. That company did quite well for itself; they just signed up their millionth distributor last year. But now you've got an endless number of juice companies that are all selling juice wholesale for $50-$60 dollars a bottle.

Our friend Russ von Hoelscher recently told us a funny story. A group of scientists did a chemical analysis of some of these miracle juices that are for sale, the ones that will supposedly cure you of whatever ails you. Need more hair? Drink the juice. No sex appeal? Drink the juice. Whatever it is, whatever problems you're having, drink the juice! Well, the scientists discovered that there's more nutrition in the Hi-C juices you can get at the grocery store for a couple of bucks. I thought that was hilarious! Chris Lakey has tried some of these expensive juices — and he tells me that they all taste disgusting, no matter how good they may be for you. Maybe these really are good products; I don't know. But I do know that nobody wants to pay $50 for a bottle of juice. They really don't.

The point is, **there are just too many of these "me too" companies out there, and their products are, well, crap.** There's a reason there are so few, if any, non-MLM companies selling these products: **because there's no real market outside of the company itself.** In other words, the only reason anyone buys the product is because they have to in order to get involved with the opportunity. **Now, with CLUB-20 International, there are a whole bunch of companies with exactly the types of opportunities we offer.** Just do Google searches on consulting services, marketing consulting services, advertising services, and things like that. Those are the kinds of things we provide, and you'll find that there are a whole lot of non-MLM companies selling them.

We have a coaching program available. We have a monthly newsletter and some other information of value that we deliver to people as part of our coaching program. We've got our Wealth Explosion Seminar. **So you're buying items you don't have to stock in inventory, unlike those other MLM opportunities.** With those, really, what you're buying is inventory to sell — and they have a rule that you have to sell 70% of the inventory you accept. You have no choice; somehow you're supposed to go out and retail 70% of the product you're sent. Well, very often that doesn't happen. It sits on shelves and it expires. And then, eventually, you have to just throw it away and pay for it yourself.

That's how it goes with the products and services no one really wants. But the marketing services we sell, like our Wealth

Explosion Seminar, are valuable services to the marketplace we sell to. They're not going to fill your garage, so that your spouse gets mad at you because she can't park her car anymore. That's one of the great things about our Wealth Explosion Seminar. There are no products to stock or ship or anything like that; you don't even have to buy one yourself. **You're simply selling a ticket to an event that people can register for and attend.** Now, we'll dump a lot of material on their heads when they come; we make it very much worthwhile to come to one of our seminars. **We give you all kinds of free gifts, products and services, so you'll go home with a big stack of stuff.** But it's not something where you're paying and paying, and every month another package of stuff is coming to you, and you have to keep piling it up.

The types of services we sell are all aimed at teaching people Direct-Response Marketing, which is a fascinating subject. We've been doing it for 20 years. The more I know about Direct-Response Marketing, the more I want to know — it's an exciting form of marketing. We're constantly learning new things and helping other people get in on that. People actually use the ideas that we share with them, and they want to know more.

PROBLEM NUMBER TEN: **Most business opportunities force you to become a salesperson.**

There are many, many great opportunities available out there... but too often, when you do a little digging, you find out that even though they offer a wonderful product that many people want, it's completely up to you to sell it. **That becomes a problem, because most people aren't salespeople.** Even those of us who are don't like to sell — or at least, we don't like to spend our time working *directly* to make a sale. **We think a better solution is putting together automated systems that do all the work for you, so you avoid the hassles and headaches**

122

of becoming a salesperson. The truth is, people would rather sit in a dentist's chair and get a couple teeth pulled than to spend that same amount of time on the phone trying to pitch something to somebody.

As you pursue opportunities, you'll note that a particular opportunity either **a)** comes with an automatic turnkey solution or **b)** you have to put together your own system. The best opportunities follow the first solution: they've already put together an automated system for you, which is ideal, because **then you're jumping right in from Day One with a system that works, one that you can easily use and replicate.** If you don't have a system already put together for you, and you don't want to become a salesperson, your only other option is to try to put one together on your own. Maybe you're a great copywriter; maybe you can write your own ads and sales letters. But if you're not, or you're uncomfortable with that, you're up the creek.

So you want to look for opportunities that have some kind of automated system built into them so you don't have to worry about becoming a salesperson, as most opportunities require you to do. While it may be true, as the saying goes, that "everything you want can be found just beyond your comfort zone," when it comes to selling — especially personal selling — there are some people who just can't. Active salespeople have to push themselves way beyond their comfort zone constantly in order to do what they do. I would encourage you to live by that quote, by the way; **push yourself some, and see where it leads you.** I've always been surprised by where doing that led me. But having said that, when it comes to opportunities and making money really fast, it's in your best interest to look for those automatic selling systems, because **they can help put money in your pocket quickly.** *Then* you can strike out beyond your comfort zone. It's always easier to push yourself a little further when you've got a bank roll.

Nobody makes any money in any opportunity until and unless something is sold. Well, we've got that well in hand at CLUB-20 International. Drew Hanson, our Sales Manager, has built a top-notch department that helps you stay in your comfort zone until you're ready to leave it. That department is small at the moment — it consists of seven full-time salespeople as of this writing — but it's growing. And it's already sold more than 200 tickets to the Wealth Explosion Seminar. **They're *proven* to be effective.** Those people really work hard, and we work hard to encourage them. It's tough work. But that's kind of the point; these guys bust their humps selling so you don't have to. They're here to help you, and us, make money.

PROBLEM NUMBER ELEVEN: **Most opportunities pay you small sums of money and no residual income.**

We've touched on this before, especially in regards to the Acid Test Formula in Chapter 1. Again, look at the ratio between how much it costs to get involved and how much is really paid out; that's a quick indicator as to how long it's going to take to make money for you and where that money's going. We keep going back to Network Marketing again and again, because there are so many examples in that field where the pay plans look good at a glance — but with a closer look, you realize they pay out big only if you get a humongous downline below you. They don't really pay you much on the front-end. So it's a good habit to get past the fluff and the hype of the compensation plan and look into the meat of it.

Your bills come in every month, like clockwork. So you need money that comes in reliably every month to pay those bills, money you can count on. That's where residual income comes in. As one of our partners, Chris Morrison, always says: **"If a business opportunity doesn't have residual income built into it... forget it."** I like that philosophy.

<u>PROBLEM</u> <u>NUMBER</u> <u>TWELVE</u>: **Most opportunities are not timely**.

This is crucial, and here's an analogy I think works well to explain it, courtesy of Kent Sayre. He took a surfing lesson once when he visited Hawaii, and his instructor told him that at a certain point, as the wave is starting to build up, you've got to start paddling just as hard as you can so that you can be there and catch the wave at the perfect time. And then you ride it to success! If that wave starts coming, and you paddle too hard and get there too fast, then the wave just goes right by you — and you're left hanging out in the ocean. Start paddling too late, and you might get clobbered as it breaks. So if you're too early you miss it; and if you're just a little too late, you still miss it. You have to be right on the money.

This analogy really struck me as apropos, because when you're investigating business opportunities, **you want to find one that's timely. Most opportunities aren't.** Worse, they know it, and try to gloss over the fact. But an opportunity that's timely is just like catching the wave at the right time. You paddle like mad and catch it so that you can ride it to success. An opportunity that's timely can make all the difference in the world.

If an opportunity is so old that everybody and their dog has heard of it, so that everybody is promoting it, then there's no real money left in it. There's no point in trying to catch a wave that's gone past; it's gone forever, spent on the shore. Sometimes the heavy hitters have already gotten in and made all their money, and they're off into the next new thing. **On the other hand, if something is too new, then people don't understand it, they've never heard of it, and there's a lot of skepticism and resistance to it.** The wave's not here yet. **So you have to find the happy medium.** There's a point where the market is familiar with what you're offering, and it's an irresistible offer; so it's the perfect timing, and suddenly, people

125

want it.

Let me give you an example. About a decade ago, there was something called a Palm Pilot, which was like a precursor to the Blackberry. They introduced it to great fanfare, and thought everybody was going to adopt it. Well, what happened was that it fell on its face; it never really caught on. But now handheld Blackberries and iPhones are very popular, because they're timely. They're hitting at the right time. People are aware of and understand the technology, and they're ready for it. **So you want to hit in the "sweet spot," that point where it's just beyond the phase of the early adopters, but hasn't reached the critical mass.** That way, the majority of people are ready and willing to be sold.

I've already used the surfing analogy for this, but here's another good one: when you're a baseball player at bat. As the pitch is coming toward you, you have to choose when to swing. If you swing a little bit too early, you either miss or the ball doesn't go where you want. You foul out, or it ends up off in left field somewhere. If you wait too long, maybe it ends up over the foul line again. You have to time your swing just right, so that you hit the ball in fair play. And, of course, not only do you have to get the ball in play, but you have to hit it as precisely as you can. If you're a bit too high on the ball, it's going to be a little grounder, and you'll be out at first base. If you get under it too much, you'll pop it up and it'll be easy to catch. So you have to not only adjust for when you swing so that you're level left and right, but you also have to be level up and down. If any of those variables aren't exactly right, you're unlikely to score a home run. **Being off by just a little bit can make a big difference.**

There's a formula we use for timing that's almost infallible. If you can get the right offer to the right audience at the right time, using the right medium, you'll get sales. A big part of that formula is the part that goes, "at the right time." Is that audience ready to buy? You have to get to people while they're hot. You'd better be ready right then and there to take advantage of that situation, too. **This goes back to one of the basic precepts of sales, which is that you have to be ready (and willing) to ask for the money.** This is something that trips up a lot of experienced marketers, but it's absolutely necessary, and it's all about timing. When Jerry Jones, the owner of the Dallas Cowboys, was asked his secret to his success, he said, "First, I ask for the money. Second, I ask for the money. Third, I ask for the money." That's crucial to success: knowing that someone is hot, ready to buy, and then asking for the money. **One thing I like about Direct-Response Marketing is that your sales material can *always* be out there asking for the money.** And even if someone isn't ready to say "Yes!" right away, well, one of the reasons we do long-form sequences — where we send multiple direct mail packages — is so we stay in the minds of our prospects. Their situations can change, so we stay on top of them and keep asking… because even though they say "No" now, they may eventually say "Yes" if something in their life changes. **A good marketing system is going to keep the pressure on.**

What makes CLUB-20 International timely right now is the fact that, as this book goes to press, we're in pre-launch. **We're brand new. *This* is the time to get started.** However, if somebody is reading this book a few years from now, the opportunity will still be relatively new at that point, too. It's also timely in other ways. **Part of the secret to timing also has to do with catching people when *they* are ready for it… when the timing is just right for *them*.** So you're using our marketing system to give away our free book. You're letting our suppliers mail the postcards for you, or you're chasing other types of advertising, and you're reaching people at the right time, with the right type of opportunity, the right type of offer. The automated system does all of that for you.

<u>PROBLEM</u> <u>NUMBER</u> <u>THIRTEEN</u>: **Many opportunities
are too complicated for the average person.**

Let's go back again to MLM. I told you about that MLM
company that I was a distributor for twice, the one out of
Michigan. I can't name them specifically, but they've been
around forever. Both times I was a distributor of this company, I
reviewed the comp plan again and again. They tried to explain it
to me, but it was so complicated I never did understand it. So, I
mean, here I was a distributor twice, and they've got all the
breakaways and all the different BVs and the PPVs, and it's just
so mind boggling. It reminds me of the tax system — just too
complicated. **Well, the more complicated a program is, the
worse it is.** If you can't explain it to people right away, forget it.
It's bad all the way around. You almost have to be a rocket
scientist to understand some of this stuff. It's a unique language
in and of itself — and I don't get it. I've been around MLM for
30 years, and I still don't understand a lot of it.

I think that many times, they invent that jargon to separate
themselves from outsiders and to deliberately confuse people —
because there are all these different bonuses you don't
understand, and you don't really know how you can obtain
them. I just felt silly not understanding it when I'd look at a pay
plan. **I think they do that on purpose — saying that there's
the potential there to make huge sums of money,** if you can
just understand, first, how easy it is. **But if they can't write it
down on a napkin, it's too complex.** Just lay it out on the table:
tell us specifically what we have to do to make money. I would
be wary of any opportunity that used too much jargon.

I think the reason they make it really complicated is
because they make money without you. **If they can make it
confusing and complicated, then you'll be lost, without any
way to succeed, and they won't have to pay you
commissions.** It's in their best interest if you don't do anything

except kindly pay your fee and not worry about how it all works. They don't want you maxing out the compensation plan, because they make more money when you don't. **That's why you want to be in a position where the company offering the opportunity makes money when *you* make money.** If they make money by helping you, they'll make things as easy and uncomplicated as possible.

CLUB-20 International is very, very simple. Besides us, only two people get paid. Now, you would think that with a comp plan like that, there wouldn't be a lot of money in it! People think, "Wow, only two people get paid?" This is confusing to them, especially if they're experienced Multi-Levelers used to seeing these huge comp plans. For example, I was looking at a compensation plan the other day, and it was some kind of wacky, weird matrix. You needed to get a few thousand people to make a few thousand dollars a month. C'mon, now, that's outrageous. How excited can you be when you see something like that? But a lot of them *are* like that. You make a few dollars here and there, and if you build a team, if you'll get five, who get five, who get five, *ad nauseum*, over time you'll build up this huge organization, and you'll be making thousands of dollars a month.

Well, we wanted to set up our compensation plan so that only two people get paid — but you each get a thousand bucks. There's no more having to build a huge team. You can build a small team, or no team at all. You can just go out there and work the system, and get paid $1,000 every time we close a sale for you. So you can make the biggest profits in the fastest time, without having to deal with odd little formulas or unreachable bonuses that you'll never qualify for. We wanted to make it easy to understand and easy to start making money.

PROBLEM NUMBER FOURTEEN: **Most opportunities cannot be done from the comfort, privacy, and safety of**

your home.

With traditional sales jobs, you've got to be out on the road, away from home a lot; you've got to go see people directly. Other opportunities revolve around brick-and-mortar type businesses where you have to have a storefront. Well, if you have a storefront you probably have employees. You've got to go to the store every day. You open it up, you close it at night, you're doing the work while you're there. You come home at night, you're tired, and you go to sleep and wake up in the morning at 6 o'clock to get back to the store by 8 o'clock… and you do that over and over again.

Nobody wants a plain old job, right? If you could have an opportunity that allowed you to work from home and be in a position where you could get up in the morning, stay in your underwear all day if you wanted to — hopefully you'd put a robe on, just in case someone comes to the front door — wouldn't that be great? You're in your bathrobe and slippers, you go grab a cup of coffee, you check the mail, you hop on your email and you see that you've got orders coming in. If you decide you want to run to the gym to go work out for an hour, you can, because you don't have anywhere else to be. Maybe you want to go eat lunch with a friend, or a parent, or a child... you can do that, no problem. You control when and how you leave the house, because you're your own boss and you're working from home. **That's the kind of opportunity you want to look for: one that puts you in command of your time.** When you have that ultimate control of your time and freedom — because you're not chained to a desk, you're not doing something based on someone else's schedule or a store you've got to go open — you're in a much better position to enjoy the reason why you wanted to become your own boss in the first place.

One of the things we're pretty excited about is the fact that paradigms and attitudes towards home-based businesses are shifting in this country. There are so many more people now than there were 10 years ago who want a home-based business. And there are a lot more people who are saying, **"Okay, with the right technology, the right opportunity, the right company, and the right infrastructure, I can do my business from** *anywhere.***"** Maybe at some point there was a stigma to running a home-based business, but today, home businesses are more accepted and more desired. **What a great time to be in our business — and to be able to offer** *great* **opportunities with** *great* **marketing systems and** *great* **guidance to a growing audience of people dying to get some of what we have!**

Chris Hollinger tells me that this ability to operate his business from home has been a big benefit to him lately. Recently, his mother became ill and was hospitalized for 10 days, and all his siblings work every single day at traditional J-O-Bs. Chris was in a position where he was the one who was able to be there for her, the one his siblings were looking to to step up and do that because they couldn't. And he was glad and happy that he was able to do that. Had Chris still been in the classroom, being there for his mom when she needed it the most would have been difficult. But Chris works from home, so he's able to set his own schedule to a large degree. Yes, he fell behind in his work during that time, but was still able to rearrange his schedule to help her.

People become self-employed because they want freedom. And yet, most don't really buy a business; they buy a job, and the business eventually owns them and places too many demands on them. Now, if you want to run a retail storefront or travel constantly to sell your products, then great! But you're not going to be free to do what you want when you want — or when you need to.

CLUB-20 offers you the perfect balance between having a career and having personal freedom. You don't have to sacrifice your family. You can have a business that's built around your lifestyle, instead of being forced to build your lifestyle around your business. You could do this in as little as 5 or 10 minutes a day; and not only that, you don't have to be sitting in your home office. You could be on vacation or traveling, and still make money. And that's the point here: you have the freedom to do it however and wherever you want to. That's what makes it so powerful.

PROBLEM NUMBER FIFTEEN: **Most opportunities are difficult to start and to run.**

Not to beat a dead horse, **but it's crucial to find something that's easy to get started and to maintain — because it all comes down to lifestyle.** Does the opportunity fit your lifestyle, given the amount of time, effort, and desire that you have to work it? You have to ask, "What exactly do I need to do to make money?" And if you can't immediately see the answer, or if someone can't say, "Here's what you can do... and this, this, and this," then you need to look elsewhere. If they start giving you vague or evasive answers, then the opportunity to make money doesn't exist. There's not that one thing you can do to make money in that opportunity, or if there is, it's too complicated to easily grasp.

At the beginning of this book, I made the point that most people who think that they want a business really don't — **they want a cash machine.** I don't mean that in a cruel way; I understand that way of thinking very well. A business is nothing but a headache. It's a hassle. It's a nightmare, sometimes. **What people want is something that runs itself.** So how do you get that? Well, the first way to get it is to build it yourself. You have to build a marketing system, which you can do; we build marketing systems all the time. You have to build an infrastructure, make contacts with suppliers, learn all the tricks of the trade. Or, second, you can work with a partner who already has all of that built. One of the two things has to happen, or business life is going to be extremely difficult for you.

CLUB-20 offers that. It's easy to start and easy to run. Now, I could have made our start-up manual hundreds of pages long if I'd wanted to. Certainly we've had other start-up manuals that were that long, and sometimes we do that just to add credibility to the offer. **But with CLUB-20 International, you've got a very simple fast-start manual; it takes about 30 minutes to understand it.** It's easy. It lets people get started right away. There's only one step, and that's to get our free book out into as many hands as possible. And along with that book comes a 36-page Special Report, which is really a sales letter. It gets people started and tries to encourage them to eliminate the qualification process by going ahead and purchasing the flagship product.

PROBLEM NUMBER SIXTEEN: **Most opportunities do not let you make money fast enough.**

This is important, because given the choice between making lots of money quickly or making lots of money slowly, hey, **everyone's going to choose quickly.** And you may have a pressing need to make a lot of money quickly, too, so it becomes that much more urgent. Well, if you need to make a lot of money quickly, joining the wrong opportunity can really sink your ship. But getting into the right opportunity could provide all the money you need — because after all, having money solves the problems that *not* having it creates. If you can write a check to make a problem disappear, it's not really a problem; that's a very liberating mindset.

On the other hand, the wrong opportunity can suck the life out of you. Here's a good example of that: a top marketer joins an MLM program and finds that the pay structure is based upon people making no money. The idea was for them to sign up for auto-shipment of the product and to have their bank accounts drained through monthly whacks on their credit cards. The whole pay plan was based on people doing nothing at all. I think of these as leech MLMs, because all they want is to suck money out of you.

Well, this guy wrapped a world-class marketing system around this pay plan and started making huge sums of money. He was bringing in $100,000 in his second month, and he was going to bring in $200,000 the third month. But before he got to that third month... what happened? The people running the MLM said, "Whoa, we're going to go bankrupt if we actually pay this guy, because he's actually working the system. Our whole system is based upon people doing nothing at all!" So, you guessed it, they kicked him out. He didn't get paid. Meanwhile, he'd spent all this time and effort to create a world-class marketing system that was duplicable. I estimate that he got robbed of over a million dollars in this opportunity. He got no commission from it at all, because of a bad pay plan that didn't let him make any money fast enough, because he was out on the road — and that MLM was so shady that when they saw the handwriting on the wall, they kicked his feet out from under him. He appealed to the CEO, not that it helped. They had their headquarters in this huge skyscraper, where they whisked him up to the top floor. While he was in the CEO's office, he noticed that there wasn't one picture of the guy's family there; all he had was a picture of his Harley Davidson or his boat. That should have told the erstwhile distributor what he was dealing with right then and there! Incidentally, that company is almost out of business now.

Even in a traditional business, you have to build your clientele first. My good friend Ray Prieba is on his way to making $100,000 a year as a massage therapist — but it took him years to build his clientele. And now the joke is, all Ray's friends are going, "God, that Ray is so lucky!" Lucky? It took him 20 years to build his clientele! It didn't happen overnight, and that's how *most* businesses are. **But CLUB-20 International is designed so that it pays large commissions very quickly.**

PROBLEM NUMBER SEVENTEEN: **Most opportunities are too much alike.**

Most opportunities try too hard to copy each other — again, they subscribe to the old "me too" philosophy. That's bad strategy. Good marketing is, in large part, about differentiation. In other words, **there's got to be something different about your company, your opportunity that completely and totally separates it from everything else.** But too many of these opportunities just blend together.

And it's so easy to start companies these days. In some states you don't even have to tell the state you're starting a business; you just do it. In others you have to file a little registration fee, but you can still start a company easily, and you can certainly build a website very easily. So someone can have the appearance of being a big company even when they're working out of their garage. That's how you get all these "me too" companies, because the easiest way to get something up and running is just to say, "Hey, I see what they're doing. I'm going to copy it and mine's going to look just like that. It's going to be real easy." So it's good to do whatever you can do to make yourself stand out.

Let's go back to the juice companies I mentioned earlier. One company out of Salt Lake City took off, so now all of a sudden there are a couple of dozen juice companies. They're all the same, even though they try to differentiate themselves with so-called specialty fruit. Most of these companies will be gone a few years from now. The juice is chemically all the same. And, even if you're really into nutrition, you can only drink so much pricy juice and take only so many special pills and powders and potions anyway. All that comes of it is really expensive urine.

The products are bored, tired, and useless, and they taste awful. In these copycat companies, the distributors don't stand a snowball's chance in hell of making it. Most of them are going to lose everything; the best that can be expected is that the experience might be a good stepping-stone opportunity for them. Maybe they'll be able to continue to move forward.

Now, if you get involved in a company like that, one thing you can do to differentiate yourself is to come up with other things you can add to the product. Throw in some free gifts or bonuses, for example, or develop your own turnkey marketing system. **One of the things we've seen people do successfully is to take something and then add their own unique marketing twist.** They'll say, "Hey, get involved with me and my downline. Join my team and you'll get my automated system." So you can make money that way (assuming the company lets you) but you have to be a marketing expert.

When a company comes along that's successful, you can guarantee that, just like designer clothes, there'll be some knock-offs right around the corner! **And some of those knock-offs end up making a mint, because they've taken something that someone else has already tested and proven to work.** All they're doing is wrapping a better marketing plan around it, or maybe a better compensation plan, better guidance, or better support, all to make a proven plan even better. It's actually the Microsoft model. Microsoft lets other, smaller companies come in and be the revolutionaries and pioneers — and then they come in behind them and do it better.

Before you start any business, you have to realize that the marketplace is over-saturated, which means that to really succeed, you've got to have something that cuts through the clutter. **It's got to be different. CLUB-20 International is.** The whole theme behind our company is "$60,000 In 90 Days." It's hot! It's exciting! People love it. *Everybody* wants to make $60,000 in the next 90 days. We've got some radio commercials going out there right now. We've got a radio infomercial that we're getting ready to test. I have plans for Direct-Response TV. We have a strong Internet campaign. It's all aimed at $60,000 in 90 days, which is the title of my book. **It's hot. It's fresh. It's new. It's exciting. It's what people want.**

At CLUB-20 International we've got a unique compensation plan. Our products and services are proprietary. **These are unique products and services that separate us from everybody else.** Even if other people launch similar opportunities, they won't have exactly what we have.

PROBLEM NUMBER EIGHTEEN: **Most of the opportunities we research are nothing more than hype and BS**.

Consider a soda can. When it's full, it's worth something: 50 or 75 cents. But when it's empty, what's it worth? Maybe a penny or two, if you recycle it. **Well, a lot of opportunities are just empty cans.** Someone wrote a good sales letter, but there's nothing behind it: there's no plan, no product, no automated system, and nothing has been figured out... it's just hollow. **You need to look very closely at an opportunity to see what's behind it.** You might even ask to see a copy of their start-up manual first. What are you going to get when you do business with them? Is it just an empty can, or is there something in there that you can drink?

Every Sunday night my wife watches this show called "Desperate Housewives." I've seen, on some of the entertainment news programs, where they show you what's supposed to be their neighborhood, with all these big, beautiful houses. But it's a fake neighborhood. All those houses look real, the street looks real, and it all looks so genuine — and yet it's all phony. There's nothing behind it. The front is nothing but a façade. The hype is there, but what's behind the hype? Nothing.

There's an infomercial that's running right now for a program that, obviously, people are making money with; they have lots of testimonials. I watched it simply because I was paying attention to the marketing behind it all. Now, if you turn the volume down and just watch it that way, all you see is two very attractive women posing for 30 straight minutes! They decided to put these women in very skimpy outfits and had them jut their chests out the whole time, because obviously they know their target market, and they're probably getting people's attention. So what's behind that opportunity? No idea. I watched it, but I couldn't tell you anything about the opportunity. Still can't. It got people's attention, that's for sure. But is there any substance behind it? Is it real? I don't know. I was distracted. So there's another message right there about marketing! That was definitely part of their marketing scheme, wasn't it?

By now, I hope I've given you enough formulas and ideas to help you cut through that kind of hype, and **I would encourage you to review them before choosing any opportunity.** Remember, purchasing is an emotional thing. People buy while they're in the heat of the moment, and they don't put enough logic into and think through some of the things I've talked about. There are very specific reasons why CLUB-20 International is a cut above most opportunities.

PROBLEM NUMBER NINETEEN: **Most opportunities are *not* part of a growing trend.**

Finding a hot trend is critical, because what's current creates currency. **To make real money, an opportunity has to**

be part of an emerging trend. Here's a good example: Suzanne Somers and the ThighMaster. It caught on. It came along at a time when the health craze and aerobics were getting ready to explode in this country. It sold millions and millions of units. Chris Hollinger's wife bought one… and he ended up turning it into a catapult for his daughters to use to shoot things over the fence at the neighbor's kids!

At any rate, if you dig in and position yourself right in front of that breaking wave, it can really put a lot of money in your pocket — especially if you can add something exciting that grabs people's attention. **It all goes back to the idea of the unique selling proposition.** What's different about you, your company, your products, and your services? What's different about your offer? What's different about your opportunity? Very often, the answer is: nothing! So you have to create that difference. But a lot of companies *haven't* created one. If you're looking at an opportunity and they haven't taken the time to create something that's exciting and really gets people's attention, then you should probably stay away from it.

So stick to emerging trends — but avoid things that are too faddish. Sure, you could make money one year, and then end up holding the bag as the fad fades away. Imagine how you'd feel right now if you'd invested a fortune in Pogs back in the 1990s. Remember those? Probably not — it was a fad that didn't last long.

You've got to be involved in opportunities where there's a growing, long-term demand. **With CLUB-20 International, we're serving the two marketplaces** I've talked about previously. In the first, there are **30-50 million small business owners** looking for a way to make more money, to be more competitive, to attract more of the best prospective buyers within their market, to retain more of those buyers — and that's what we help them do. And then there are all the **Baby Boomers** who are retiring or getting ready to, and who know that there's not going to be quite enough money left over at the end of the month. They're looking for a way to supplement their income, or become financially independent — or maybe they just want something to do that doesn't involve sitting in front of the TV. That's what my Dad did when he retired. He immediately plunked himself down in his recliner and started watching TV all the time. I said, "Dad, you've got to quit watching so much TV!" Well, he said he was watching the Discovery Channel and the Learning Channel and such, so he wasn't really watching TV — he was learning stuff all day. But come on — when you do that, you're still just sitting on your butt all day long watching TV. The point is, most people find out that retirement isn't all it's cracked up to be, and then they need something to do. Well business like this is more than just about making money. It's about doing something that you're interested in and passionate about.

I talked about riding a wave on a surfboard earlier in the chapter. Well, if you get too far out in the ocean, you'll find that there's no wave; you're ahead of the trend. And if you wait till the wave is almost all the way up to shore, it's real tiny, and it's too late. So there's a right time to catch a wave. **You want to catch it on the growing trend, like we offer with CLUB-20.** We're going to see a skyrocketing growth as Baby Boomers retire. This is an industry that's going to explode as more and more Baby Boomers start looking for ways to supplement their retirement income and allay their boredom. As this wave of Boomers hits, business opportunities are going to see huge growth — especially the ones, **like CLUB-20 International, where there's already a track record of success.**

PROBLEM NUMBER TWENTY: **Most opportunities are not unique.**

Imagine walking through a huge bookstore, with thousands of books on the shelves... but they're all the same. I imagine

140

you'd very quickly get bored once you realized it didn't matter which one you picked. Or suppose you had 10 McDonald's restaurants in a row, and you loved eating burgers, and you were hungry for lunch. Well, what difference does it make if you choose this McDonald's, or that McDonald's, or the McDonald's over there? They're all the same. That's analogous with what you're facing in the opportunity world. There's so much hype, hot air, fluff, and empty showmanship. It's all sizzle and no substance — so much so, that customers are more skeptical than ever. They're confused, and they want to get to the reality and figure it out. **An opportunity that's unique, that differentiates itself in the marketplace, is going to thrive.**

So let's go back to that bookstore, where all those thousands of books are the same. Now, if there was *one* book that was different, I think you would gravitate towards it. Why? **Because of the differentiation.** It's the Law of Contrast. We're looking for differences in a world where everything is the same, and we just can't tell the difference between all those things. The thing that sticks out the most is what we gravitate towards.

So you want to make sure that the opportunity you join is unique, and here's how you do that: **look for someone who gives you a straightforward, no-hype answer.** Just ask whoever's promoting the opportunity this question: "What's different about you and your opportunity that's going to make me want to do business with you, as opposed to all those other options, including the option of doing absolutely nothing at all?" Here's where you have to pierce through the hype and just get a factual answer. If they start stammering and stumbling, and can't clearly articulate what makes this one different from all the rest, then there's no unique selling proposition, and it's an opportunity that's hard to market.

You've got to make sure the opportunity is unique before moving forward. You're looking for things that are new,

141

exciting and different. That's really what people want: something new. People are addicted to the new. For example, every time I call my Mom, the first thing I say is, "What's new?" We don't want to hear about stuff we've talked about 40 million times, even though we always end up talking about it anyhow. We're trying to see if, my God, is there something *new*? Most of the time the answer is "No."

PROBLEM NUMBER TWENTY-ONE: **Most opportunities force you to do everything on your own.**

It's as if they've given you a 10,000 piece jigsaw puzzle. There are all these different pieces, and they just throw them all on the floor, and you've got to put it all together yourself — assuming you can find all the pieces. It's complicated. It's confusing. **So once again, you have to look for companies that have a vested interest in helping you succeed.** Do they make a significant portion of their profits based on the money they make for you? If the answer is "No!," then stay away from it!

Let's go back to franchises. I've told you about the folks in Hesston, Kansas, who paid $125,000 for a coffee shop. One reason is because it's a franchise, so they were paying money for something that's proven. The company behind that franchise provides all kinds of support services as part of what they got for that $125,000. They have Regional Managers and all these different meetings they can go to, and ongoing training, and all kinds of things where they're doing everything possible to help them succeed. **At CLUB-20, you've got all the help you need, too.**

PROBLEM NUMBER TWENTY-TWO: **Most business opportunities will never make you rich.**

How do you define "rich"? Some people would be happy with an extra $1,000 a month, and some people would be happy with $5,000 or $10,000 a month, and some people get upset if they make less than $100,000 a month. So the definition of "rich" depends on what you want; you define what "rich" is for you. That can be very subjective. I remember watching "60 Minutes" in the mid-1980s when Mike Wallace interviewed Bunker Hunt. That was when Bunker and his brother were trying to corner the silver market, and Mike Wallace said to him, "How much do you make?" And Bunker wouldn't say anything. So Mike asks, "A million a day?" And Bunker Hunt, real snobbishly, replies, "I'd starve to death if I made a million dollars a day." Of course, he and his brother just about went broke later on.

In any case, most opportunities won't let you become anywhere near what you would consider rich or extremely wealthy. **The problem usually lies in either the compensation plan, if it's MLM, or the profit margin of the product you sell.** There are a lot of MLM companies that pay you a few dollars on every sale. Now they tell you, "Just build it high and deep and wide, and pretty soon you'll have 30,000 people. And even though you're only making a buck on each sale, you make so much money every month because you bring in so many people." Well, most people never are able to do that.

You have to look out for these distributorship opportunities. Sometimes they sell inexpensive products; the products may be really great, but they sell them for a low price. So maybe they sell a product for $40 and you get half of that. Well, yeah, that can add up. But even over the long term, that kind of profit won't make you wealthy. It probably isn't going to provide a lifetime income. Now, maybe you make $20 on the initial sale, and they've got some kind of back-end slack adjuster product that makes you big profits; just because your first sale is a $20 profit doesn't mean there aren't other things in place to make you more money. **But you've got to be wary of any**

opportunity that doesn't have some kind of ability to make a lot of money, some kind of big ticket priced item to help you with your marketing costs and provide you a good healthy long-term profit. If it can't make you huge amounts of money, well, there are better opportunities out there. As one of the guys that helped us out in the beginning used to say, "You've gotta sell a lot of 99-cent tacos if you want to make millions of dollars." And I like that; I never forgot it.

No matter how good an opportunity is, if the market for it is too small or the products and services aren't sold for enough money, that in and of itself will limit you. **That's why you've got to find opportunities where there's a big market, where there's a lot of demand within that marketplace;** it's a growing market, so there's some future there, a surety there that it's going to be something long-term. Then too, **the products and services need to sell for enough profit, and there needs to be enough repetition involved in the sale so that people will re-buy again and again. CLUB-20 International has all of those.**

PROBLEM NUMBER TWENTY-THREE: **Most moneymaking opportunities do not pay you the largest percentage of upfront cash.**

You absolutely have to have that large percentage of upfront cash to really make a go of things, because if not, it's just not going to add up for you — especially if you're spending a lot of money on your own advertising and marketing, or building an infrastructure. **So there's got to be some nice profit right away.** Marketers like us can't operate on low percentages, simply because of the money that we spend in fulfillment costs, mailing costs, and advertising costs. The numbers have to be there. You don't want to operate on a shoestring budget. Now, we're involved in a few MLM companies we're excited about that don't pay large sums of upfront cash, but they're not our primary income source either. **For primary income, you need something like that huge $1,000 payout that CLUB-20 International offers whenever you or one of your team members makes a sale.**

PROBLEM NUMBER TWENTY-FOUR: **Most business opportunities are filled with gaps and missing pieces.**

I view evaluating a business opportunity as being much like you'd evaluate a car before you bought it. For example: my colleague Kent Sayre tells me that the very first car he ever bought, he evaluated all wrong — meaning he just looked at the outside. It looked shiny and neat, so he didn't get a mechanic's inspection, didn't even look under the hood, barely test drove it — and it turned out to be a real lemon. He didn't have a lot of money at the time, and it ended up nickel-and-diming him to death. But hey, it looked hot! Kent looked good in it! It got so bad that the brakes were running thin, and he couldn't get them fixed. The brakes actually stopped working in the middle of an intersection, because he didn't have the money to fix them! But the car looked good. He looked good as he ran right out there into the middle of the intersection, his life flashing before his eyes. Fortunately he was able to hit the emergency brake and get it stopped — but his mechanic told him he should have been dead, and he really chastised Kent for waiting that long. All that could have been prevented, had he paid for a good mechanic's inspection and looked underneath the hood.

So how does that tie in to business opportunities? Well, when you're looking at an opportunity, you need to kick the tires, check the brakes and oil, and see if the person on the other end has worked as hard or harder on delivery and fulfillment as they have on the actual marketing to get you involved. That's critical. I've met marketers who spend about 98% of their thought on how to sell their opportunity, and maybe 2% of the time on how to actually fulfill the promises to you, the customer.

So you want to look underneath the hood and examine the engine in depth, and you want to do this in a hype-free, very logical, rational way. Look for the right checkpoints, and if it matches up, hey, you've got a good engine here; this is a business opportunity to get involved in. Don't be like Kent, who bought a car that looked good but almost killed him. **You want to stay away from business opportunities that are full of gaps and missing pieces, where the fulfillment just isn't there.** That's a recipe for disaster, because even if you do everything that you're supposed to, you won't make money.

Here's another good automotive example. Chris Lakey once bought a car from CarMax, the Wal-Mart of used car dealers; they've got them all over the U.S. You go in there and the price they have is the price you pay; it's supposedly an easier way to buy a car. He had a fine experience buying a car from them, but the important thing is this: in their showroom, they have two cars sitting there that look identical. One of them has been totaled and rebuilt to look right, but the frame underneath is all bent up, but you'd never know that, because to look at it, it looks exactly like the one that was never in a wreck. That's a graphic way of showing that you need to be careful when you buy a car, because you never know what you're buying. Your car could be completely rusted out on the inside — but someone did a quick paint job, and made it look nice on the outside. **So you've got to know what you're looking for.**

Again, it's the same thing with an opportunity. **You have to look beyond the surface so you can figure out if there are any missing parts.** You may be a great marketer, but if something in the system isn't working right, it'll throw everything out of whack. It's sort of like an electrical line. Now, I'm no electrician, but I know that if there's one short in the system, the whole thing won't work. And it can be a really small problem, too; old Christmas lights are a good example. Today, they make them so that one can go out, and the rest of them will still work. But it used to be that, if one bulb went out, the whole strand wouldn't work. Well, with a marketing opportunity, you have to go through and try out each little "bulb." Just one problem in the entire system can cause you severe headaches and prevent you from making as much money as you ought to.

So many opportunities just make their money by selling the opportunity, plain and simple. They want you to figure everything out for yourself, because they're not incentivized to help you; all the pieces you need to succeed aren't there, and there's no support, guidance, or help of any kind. You're on your own. **Well, with CLUB-20 International you're in business for yourself, but never *by* yourself. The pieces are all there.** We're here to help you, to support you. In fact, we'll do a lot of it for you, because we earn the bulk of our profits by helping you earn money.

PROBLEM NUMBER TWENTY-FIVE: **Most business opportunities are loaded with problems, headaches and hassles.**

People get started on a new opportunity with the best of intentions. Their hopes are high; they've got the dream of starting their own business — but it quickly turns into a nightmare. I run into people all the time who used to be self-employed, and when I start talking to them about it, they say the same thing my Mom says to me about the business she was in for 15 years: "Thank God I'm out of that!"

My Mom loves children, and so one day she talked my step-dad into starting a daycare business. They were in it for 15 years, and at one point, had a hundred kids in their center, along with 20-25 full-time employees. She started it because she loves children, but for 15 years, her job had very little to do with the kids and a lot do with her being a babysitter, meeting state quotas and dealing with minimum-wage employees who fought all the time. Can you imagine having 25 women fighting all around you for 15 years? Then add all the state regulatory problems, with the inspectors constantly coming in all the time. My Mom's center was located in a poor area of town, so most of her clientele had their child care paid for by the government. Let's just say they weren't the very best clientele and leave it at that. The little kids would come in dirty, not fed right; the only decent food they got was provided by her business.

I think it's indicative of a lot of businesses. People get started in them for all the right reasons. My Mom loves children, so now she's a nanny and loves every minute of her job. She's got three little kids to care for, she works for one family, and she's in Heaven! It's just a wonderful experience — every day is paradise for her! She doesn't have all the employees or the paperwork. All the rules and regulations are gone. No more state inspectors, or worse. There was a time when one of the parents complained to the local TV station, and camera crews came to her daycare center. She didn't want her kids to be filmed, so there she was, chasing away these cameramen. On the "NEWS AT 5," here's my Mom — one of the most honest people I have ever met — on display like she's some kind of shady criminal, because she's chasing off the cameras.

Look, most businesses are just a pain in the neck. You've got employees, you've got too many headaches, too many hassles. **You've got to look for a business that *doesn't* have all that. I think the lesson here is that you have to look at all the angles before you buy.** My Mom wanted to just love on kids and have a daycare; it was all about the kids. And then she got blindsided by all the bureaucratic stuff that goes along with it. There are a lot of businesses like that; you decide you want to do something, and so you get into that business, and then you find out there's all this other stuff that goes along with it. **So you**

have to look at the sum of everything you're getting into.
What are all the other problems or challenges that you'll face
with this opportunity or industry? There are good and bad points
to just about any business. So consider everything when you're
looking at an opportunity, because there *will* be problems. There
may be pain and frustration, even in little business opportunities
like the one my Mom was involved with for 15 years.

What people really want and need are the benefits that a
business provides, without all of the nightmares and
infrastructure problems. A business can be very demanding, and
if that's what you want, go for it! **But if you're like everyone
else, and are looking for the benefits without the heartache,
you should sign up for CLUB-20.**

PROBLEM NUMBER TWENTY-SIX: **Most business
opportunities require huge sums of money to get started.**

I've already covered this to some extent, but it bears
repeating. When you open a retail store, you have to buy or lease
a storefront and pay for all the expenses that go with it. Before
you bring in your first dollar, you've got to lay out a bunch of
cash. Buying into a franchise is the same way. You could pay
$100,000 in franchise fees just to get your logo on the building.
To say that you're a McDonalds costs, I think, around
$1,000,000 or so. There are all kinds of franchises that are a lot
less expensive, but even with some smaller franchises, you
might spend $15,000-$50,000 dollars just to buy the right to use
their logo and their signage.

So when you're evaluating an opportunity, **look at the
start-up costs.** There are all kinds of other variables that you
want to consider. Do you have to pay a licensing fee? How
much is that fee? What do you get in return? Do you get an
automated system? Do you get some kind of help and support?
What about inventory? Is there stuff you have to ship and

package? Do you need warehouse space? Will they drop-ship, if it's a product you're buying a license for? All those things add up and are costs that, in many cases, you have to incur before you even get started. Many opportunities end up nickel-and-diming you to death. So know what you're getting going into it. Maybe you can absorb those costs. If you're looking at an opportunity, and it's going to cost you $10,000 to really get it off the ground, well, what are you getting for that? What kind of position is that going to put you in? Maybe it's okay. Maybe it's worthwhile to spend the $10,000 because of what you're getting in return. Maybe it's not.

A lot of opportunities that cost a lot to get started have all the other problems I've already mentioned. But certainly, some good opportunities are not cheap, and in many cases, you get what you pay for. So I'm not saying not to spend a lot of money on an opportunity. **I'm saying that you need to make sure of what you're getting before you spend that money.** Know where your money's going and what you're getting in return, and then you can decide whether that's a good thing to spend your money on.

Kent Sayre has a relative who started up a Mexican food restaurant. They thought that because they understood how to cook a good burrito, taco, or quesadilla in their home, that they could build a business doing that. They shelled out $50,000 just to rent the space, buy all the equipment, and hire employees. And the problem is, they have no marketing system right now, so it's very difficult for them, and they're barely covering their bills. They're trying to make up for that $50,000 by selling $7 burritos. That's going to be very hard to do. So they're already in the red, and they're going to have to really work hard and try to be positive. It's just a real difficult situation, because they have to sell so much just to get to break even, much less to get into profits.

And then there's the whole idea that customers are going to just come back automatically. I think that's a delusion a lot of businesspeople have; **they're not even keeping a customer list, and so they have no marketing system and no control.** They think that business is like *Field of Dreams*: "if you build it, they will come." But what they're facing is the harsh awakening that they've got the food, but people are not coming. They need to pound the pavement and get people in. Kent tries to tell them that, but he's just that relative they see at Christmas parties. He's not a marketing guy in their eyes. They wouldn't listen to him anyway; he's a prophet in his own hometown, so to speak.

The point is, most opportunities cost far too much to get started in, whereas with CLUB-20, you can start for less money than you'd pay for a good used car. Of course, a lot of people argue about what that means: what does a good used car sell for? Somebody told me recently they can get a good used car for $500, and I said, "Well, all right — but *I* wouldn't want to take it on the road!" Heck, I wouldn't want to take even a $5,000 car on the road cross-country without having a mechanic really look it over.

The thing about CLUB-20 is that there's no cost for the basic distributor position, other than the $97 annual fee. So, technically, you can get started without spending much money at all — just $97 a year for the distributor kit and membership, which gets you your website and everything you need to start making money. **On the other hand, you can buy your own seminar ticket for a few thousand and instantly be qualified.** Of course, even if you just become a basic distributor, you're going to want to spend some money on advertising.

So let's say that you can get started in CLUB-20 for around a few thousand dollars (however you wanted to look at it). **That's still dirt-cheap,** compared to businesses that require you to either buy a franchise and spend $15,000, $20,000 or even more, or where you have to spend $100,000 to open a store front. There are all kinds of expensive ways to get started in business. Just look in the newspaper to prove it to yourself. Any weekend newspaper has businesses for sale, and even though the prices aren't always advertised, you'll see enough that are. You can see it's very expensive.

I've mentioned that my best friend's got a pest control business in Wichita, Kansas, and she paid $575,000 for that business. She paid more than *half a million* for a bug-killing business! Of course, it was an established 20-year-old company with a very good reputation, but that's a heckuva lot of money!

And now, drum-roll please… PROBLEM NUMBER TWENTY-SEVEN: **Most business opportunities are very risky.**

I've already done a lot of elaborating on just how risky businesses can be. Obviously, you face risk every time you get up in the morning and step out onto your front porch. A meteorite could strike you. You might get hit by a bus on the way to work. It's risky because there are so many things you can't take into account. **But despite the risk, there are a lot of rewards out there as well.** When you've done your homework and you've found that new opportunity that's on the verge of explosion — one that has all the right elements of guidance and support and compensation so that everything falls into place — you just know it when you see it, especially when you get in the habit of continually evaluating business opportunities. **And it helps to eliminate the risk when you can go through this litmus test of what makes it strong, what makes it weak, what makes it risky.** Any business, whether it's franchise, Network Marketing, affiliate, brick-and-mortar, or online will have its inherit risks. Your money is on the line.

The ones to avoid are the ones where you add all of the

problems together, you think it through, and it just spells risk. The more expensive an opportunity is, the more unproven it is, the smaller the niche, and the more it's based on something that's faddish in nature, the more risky it is. **Now, there's no such thing as a risk-free business; anybody who tells you that** is simply lying. **But there are things you can do to minimize your risk, and that's what all smart entrepreneurs and business owners do.** That's the name of the game. When you have all of the right elements in place, you're able to do that.

Any opportunity that can pay you huge sums of up-front cash, where you're involved with partners who make the bulk of their money by helping you make money, and it's all set up to pay you fast eliminates the risk. **All the things that have gone into CLUB-20 International help you eliminate the risk.** Does that mean that there's not any risk? No. There's no such thing. All business is managed risk. That's why you hear people say, "Don't get into business unless you can afford to risk the money that you're spending." What you want to do is do everything possible to accentuate the positive things that I've talked about, and eliminate anything negative. If you're able to do that, you have the closest thing you can find to a risk-free business.

Earning money is risky, because you might not be able to keep it. And certainly the government takes about half of it, so earning money is risky in that respect, too. But again, the idea is to limit risk so that when people choose to get involved in your opportunity the risk is as small as possible. **With CLUB-20, we not only have guarantees when you buy your seminar ticket, but we put together automated systems so that we can control as much as we can by not leaving you to figure everything out on your own.** We put you in the best position to make money. We can't guarantee that anybody *will*, because there are all kinds of variables beyond our control. But we try to put you in position to limit your risk.

We can't control who buys our product, but we can guarantee it. If someone comes to us, buys our product and then says after they get it, "You know, I've looked everything over. This just doesn't seem like it's a good match for what I'm looking for," well, **they can get their money back, no questions asked.** So we reverse the risk, even though there's risk inherently there, and make it as easy as possible for people to check it out without any risk or obligation. **They can get their money back if it's not right for them — all the way up to halfway through the seminar they've purchased.** All they have to do is walk up to any of our staff members and say they want their money back, and we immediately write them a check. **If they're not happy, we're not happy.**

All that is part of the risk-reversal process. We want to make it as easy as possible for people to check out our opportunity, get involved with us, and if they're not happy for whatever reason, they can get their money back when they come to the event. Again, the event is what they're paying for. The distributor position is actually free when you buy your own seminar ticket, so there's no money to get back buying the opportunity.

We've taken the best of the best of everything that we've done since 1988, everything we've used to generate more than $100 million in total revenue in our first 20 years, and we've poured it into CLUB-20 International. It really is the best of the best.

Now, let me tell you a little story about Randy Hamilton, one of our Vice-Presidents. He's our accountant guy over at M.O.R.E., Inc.—the money man, so to speak — and he's been with the company almost for the entire 20 years. Of course, we didn't find out this until later, but soon after he first started working for us back in 1989, he looked at what we were selling and said, "Man, I've got to find another job, because there's no way that this company is going to last." And then he forgot about it. About a month later he thought, "Man, I'd better get my resume out there. This company just isn't going to last. There's no way!" We were selling that little *Dialing For Dollars* publication at the time. And then he'd forget about it and go back to work; we had plenty of work to do. About six months later, it was the same thing: "Randy, you'd better get yourself out there and get a real job." I'm sure he and his wife talked about it at night. And then it became once a year: "God, this company can't last. How long can this company last?"

Well, the joke is on Randy! He's been here since 1989. And what has sustained us for 20 years? First of all, he didn't understand the market that we were in, and now he does. **It's the market that's driven; it's the market that drives every business.** We have a hungry market out there full of people with a heartfelt desire to make money. That's part of what this country is all about. It's part of the reason that other people in other countries are attracted to this great nation. **All of the products and services in CLUB-20 International are built around those same marketplaces we've been serving — the same marketplaces that have generated millions of dollars for us.** Now the best of the best has all been incorporated together into this one opportunity. Although many people, and all good business opportunity promoters, claim that they have something that's the best, **we really do have it; and hopefully you'll be able to see that.** Get beyond the emotion of it, and just see that, logically, this is the business opportunity that you've been searching for all your life. Get involved, and you'll feel great about what we're doing.

PART TWO

The 15 Main Reasons Why CLUB-20 International Has the Potential to Make You RICH!

CHAPTER FIVE:

Cranking Up the Cash Machine

I realized long ago that most people who think they want a business really don't. I sure thought *I* wanted a business, back in the day. But then I got one, and I found out that really, it's a lot of work — along with a lot of heartache, hassles, and headaches. **What I really wanted was a cash machine, and I believe that, deep down, you feel the same way.** We'd all like the ability to print money — figuratively, of course, since actually *printing* money isn't all that hard, if you've got the full capacity of a print shop behind you. What you need is something legal that will essentially do the same thing, right? A machine where you just push the button, and the money comes right out.

That's not a literal possibility, but I will say this: it's quite possible to systematize all of your marketing, all of your business, to the point where the money can come flowing in as if it were issuing from a cash machine. In fact, we develop marketing systems all the time that allow us to kick back, put our feet up, and make money with very little effort. That is the gospel truth. As ironic as it might sound, **when I look back at the last 20 years of my own life, the times when I've done the best financially have usually been the times when I've done the least amount of work.** We had a hot promotion, the marketing system was in place, and the staff and infrastructure to run our business all worked like a well-oiled machine. Everybody knew what they were supposed to do. Everybody had their job and was doing it, and the money was just flowing in. **So what we try to do is deliberately create cash systems that duplicate that effect.**

That's what we've done with our new CLUB-20 International. I know that, for a lot of people, all that sounds too good to be true — and I never blame anybody for being skeptical. In fact, I tell people quite often, especially when I meet with them one-on-one, that it's *good* to be skeptical. **You *should* be skeptical. But if you stay too skeptical too long, you'll become cynical — and that's not so good.** Cynicism can sour a person. We all know people in this world who are too cynical, and you just can't help those folks. They're bitter; they're resentful; they're skeptical; they're close-minded to everything; and they have nothing good to say about anything. So skepticism, if you stay with it too long, can turn into a negative quality. But it's good to be a *little* skeptical. If you're not a little skeptical, you're going to get taken advantage of. **That's why we encourage people to question things.** Don't just substitute our ideas for yours. *Think* about what we're saying.

CLUB-20 International is a brand new opportunity that's both evolutionary and revolutionary. **It combines the best of the best of everything that we've developed and discovered in the last 20+ years; that's the evolutionary part of it. The revolutionary part is that we're the exact opposite of most MLM companies.** Here's one quick, very specific example of how we're the exact opposite: traditional MLM companies pay small commissions that are scattered down through large groups and layers of distributors. Sure, if you build a huge downline with thousands of people in your organization, even if you're just making a small percentage on all those thousands of people, you can go to your mailbox and pull out a check for $20,000-$50,000 every month. There are people *right now* who are getting high five-figure and even six-figure checks every single month, because they've got a huge downline with thousands of people in it. If you hang in there long enough, and you work hard enough; and if you're a heavy-hitter who doesn't mind living on the road; and you can get up in front of people and motivate and inspire and fill hotel ballrooms; and do all of those kinds of things that are necessary — you *can* get rich with traditional MLM. **But most people never do, because they don't have the necessary qualities and abilities.**

The funny thing about MLM is that people make fun of it and say that it's a bunch of "get-rich-quick" hooey. **It's really not. It's more like "get-rich-slow" for most people.** You have to put a lot of work into it for it to succeed, partly because of the way that they pay you with their compensation plan. Well, CLUB-20 International is the exact opposite of that. **We pay large percentages of commission to very small groups of distributors, so we pay out more money, faster.** We put fast cash into people's pockets. They build momentum. They don't drop out. That's just one of the revolutionary aspects of our program, and one I'll discuss in more detail later.

In this half of the book, we're going to cover the 15 main reasons why CLUB-20 International has the ability to make you rich. The same methods that are making millions of dollars for one person can make millions for you, too. There are formulas you can use. There are common denominators. There are things that you can point to that every opportunity must have in order for you to get rich — and if you don't have those factors working for you, you're in trouble. **So in PART II, we're going to show you how CLUB-20 International provides fifteen of those factors — and why they're important.**

Chapter Six:

The First Five Reasons

The <u>FIRST</u> <u>REASON</u> that CLUB-20 International has the potential to make you rich is simply this: **the timing is absolutely perfect.**

We've all heard the cliché, "You've got to be involved in the right opportunity at the right time." That cliché is true to a certain extent; **timing isn't everything, but it *is* vitally important.** When you study the lives of the people who make the largest amounts of money quickly, you'll see that they were all involved in opportunities that were extremely timely in nature. I told you about our *Dialing for Dollars* program. Answering machines were still relatively new, so there was some excitement, a *buzz* about them — and we came along with a program that showed people how to make money with such a machine. That helped us make $10 million in a few short years.

Here's an analogy that I hope will help you understand this a little better. I lived in Southern California for a few years when I was a teenager. I never really learned how to surf, but I *did* learn how to body surf, and I did that a lot. The whole secret of body surfing — or any surfing, actually — is simple. You've just got to catch a wave at the right time. If you catch it too early, that's not good. If you catch it too late, then you won't get anywhere. You've got to catch it perfectly. I managed that a few times when I was body surfing. I didn't catch them all the time, but I caught a few perfect waves — and it's the most amazing thing, because the wave just takes you right in to shore. That's a good metaphor for making money.

You've got to get in front of a billion-dollar parade. You've got to look where the trends are. Timing is definitely important. **It's been said in our industry that we do well when the economy does well — and that we do even better when the economy goes south.** That's truer today than it's been in a long while. I don't want to give them a plug, but check out Legalzoom.com. They're having a rush of people looking to get legal advice on setting up home-based businesses. So what does that tell us as entrepreneurs in this industry? It tells us that there are a lot of people looking at non-traditional sources to supplement their income right now. They're looking for ways to help make ends meet or even survive in this bad economy. That really bodes well for the industry, which is why I think that the timing is so good right now and will continue to be for quite some time.

I really like the metaphor of the surfer here. There's a perfect time to catch a wave, and there are plenty of bad times before and after. If you get it too early — if you're out too far in the water — there's no wave at all, or at most you'll catch a tiny bit of the wave before it really builds momentum, and you won't be able to ride it very far. If you get it too late, you might catch the tail end of the wave and ride it a bit — or you might end up wiping out. What you need to do is time your opportunity and catch the wave at the right time, so you can ride it all the way in.

In business, you're talking about finding the right opportunity that you can catch as it's building momentum and ride to monetary success. If you wait too late, suddenly everybody already has one of those widgets that you've bought the rights to sell. It's not exciting anymore; it's old school. But you can also be too early to the marketplace, and end up ahead of your time. A good friend of ours developed something that I thought was pretty cool technology: a system that involved using Internet-capable cameras. He spent a lot of money developing it — and it didn't take off. He was too early to catch the front end of the webcam wave, when Internet video came to the forefront of people's thought. **He was just in the market too early.** To succeed that early, he would have had to dump millions of dollars into consumer education just to teach people what his product was, what the need for it was, and why his product helped solve that need — because it wasn't commonplace.

So to catch the perfect wave at the right time means you can't be too early, and you can't be too late. Now, you may have been in a stadium, or have seen on TV, where they did the Wave, and it went all the way around the stadium. They still do it every now and then. But have you ever been at a stadium when some guy wanted to get the wave started, and it was like a dead firecracker? Where everybody around him was like, "What is this guy doing?" Basically, how this relates to timing is in how you really get a Wave started in a stadium. You have to talk to the people around you and say, "Hey, let's start the Wave." You have to get enough people in it so that it takes on a life of its own. Right now, Chris Lakey, Chris Hollinger, my other friends, and I are sitting in the CLUB-20 International stadium saying, "Hey, look, we're going to start this Wave, and this is how we're going to do it, and it's going to go all the way around. It's going to be really cool!" And you, and all the other readers like you, are the ones who are sitting next to us right now. You're able to go "1, 2, 3... wooo!" and then it takes off! **We're creating some real momentum right now!**

With *Dialing for Dollars*, the money came pouring in because we had the right opportunity at the right time, and we introduced it to the right people. And it's really as simple as that. We did the same thing with the Internet. In 1994, we were right there in the very beginning when everything was still brand new... when just the term "the Internet" was exciting! **And with**

CLUB-20 International, again, we take MLM and turn it on its head. Now, when I get involved in something, I go out and get all the books I can on the subject. Almost 30 years ago, when I first got involved in MLM, if you wanted a book on the subject, you had to do it through mail order. It wasn't a popular subject back then; but nowadays MLM is everywhere. You can go to any bookstore and find books about MLM. In addition, enough people have tried MLM and failed, so there are a lot of frustrated MLM distributors out there. In fact, some people would say that almost every MLM distributor is at least a little frustrated on some level — and I would tend to agree.

The bottom line is, **CLUB-20 International is a whole new type of MLM company.** We're not the first to use this method of compensation. As I mentioned in Part I, we discovered it several years ago, when we got involved in an opportunity that generated about a million dollars for us before we started having problems with the company. We've adopted a modified version of this comp plan, and we've tried to solve the problems that are inherent to all other MLM companies. I think we've done that in an excellent, profitable way. **This is part of what makes the timing so exciting: the fact that we're solving a lot of problems in the marketplace.**

In addition, **all our products and services are designed to help people make more money.** As you know, our flagship product is a three-day Wealth Explosion Seminar. We have coaching programs as part of our product line, too. **Those programs are designed to help people make money with the same strategies and methods we've used to generate our fortune.** Again, we're serving two markets here. The first is the estimated 30-50 million small business owners in America — that is, people with companies that employ fewer than 50 people. **We're teaching them Direct-Response Marketing,** which is a uniquely profitable form of marketing that's widely known and just as widely misunderstood. A lot of people think Direct-Response Marketing is just mailing letters or postcards. They don't understand all of the dynamics behind it. It's complicated at times — and it's our passion.

Our goal is to help these small business owners make more money. Most of them are struggling, due to a combination of factors. A big part of it is increased competition. Some of the emerging technological trends have made it easier for people to get into business now than ever before. Another part of it is because **traditional advertising methods just don't work that well anymore.** The modern consumer has almost a built-in aversion to advertising. Let me use a metaphor to explain that.

As I've mentioned, my best friend has had a pest control business for the last six or seven years. I've helped her do her marketing, so I know a lot about the pest control business. One of the things that they do in pest control is that when they treat people's homes on their monthly contracts, they use a different poison every month. They have to keep track, and they have to keep changing their poisons constantly. Why? Because if you keep shooting the same poison month after month, the bugs just build up an immunity to it, and it stops killing them.

This may be a terrible analogy, but the point is that people these days have built up an immunity to most traditional advertising. We're numb to it; we don't even think about it; and at a conscious level at least, it doesn't affect us anymore. That's part of the challenge that all small businesses have. There are marketing methods that correct all that. **Direct-Response is an especially powerful form of marketing, because very few people understand it.** Those who do understand it have a real advantage over all of those who don't. **And so, one of our markets here is extremely timely.** All those business people need to make more money, but they don't understand anything about Direct-Response Marketing.

Ruthlessly done, Direct-Response Marketing can help you take the cream of the crop out of your market and leave your competitors scrambling after the scraps. That's timely to any business owner who's struggling, who wants to capture more market share, who wants to be more competitive, who wants to make more money for himself, his business, his employees and his family. **It works regardless of product or service.** Now, would that be attractive to business owners? Of course! That's why our products help position you in front of that wave of people who really need this information.

One of the flaws that I think is common to business owners is that they're good at doing whatever it is they do, but they're not so good at being marketers. **They have no clue how to market, so one of two things happens.** Either they stay bad at marketing and suffer because of it, or they outsource it to other companies like ad agencies that really have no interest in helping them succeed. Ad agencies only want to get their advertising dollars. And often, they have flawed systems, too. There are some good ones out there, but most just specialize in what they call "brand awareness" or "image awareness." They just want to get your name out there. They don't really understand Direct-Response Marketing, so if you spend $10,000 a month on advertising, they'll use that money to buy all kinds of brand awareness ads. They'll run ads on TV and the radio. They're not Direct-Response-driven ads, though. They just talk about your product or your company. They tell funny stories. They have you look goofy on camera.

Chris Lakey used to work for a car company, and he has a frightening story about how a bad ad agency can hurt a company. This horrible agency got ahold of the owner of the car company, and the ads that he ran on TV were just *stupid*. Chris believes that this was because the people at the agency had no clue about how to really drive business. Now, Chris never saw the numbers, so maybe those ads worked — but they just seemed silly. The owner would go on TV and do funny things. That was it. It was just him in front of a camera, and he really didn't talk about his business or why you should visit that particular dealership. Then, at the end, their website and 800-number would flash on the screen, and that was it. That kind of thing really doesn't do a lot to directly drive traffic.

When it comes to Direct-Response for a local business, we're talking about doing things like sending people coupons that they can bring into the store and use immediately. We're talking about giving prospects a special offer they have to respond to in order to get a free report that tells them why they should do business with you. **A lot of businesses never think of simple things like that.** Instead, they work with ad agencies that run image awareness ads that don't really tell you why you should do business with that company. They give you no benefits, no offers. And so a company is left going, "Well, business is okay, but I don't really know if it could be doing any better." Or, "Business is down, but I've got this ad agency working for me, so something must be working. But I don't have a clue what is and what isn't." So we teach Direct-Response Marketing. **Local businesses can benefit from this, because they can see a direct result when they run their ads.** They can know right away whether their advertising works. We put our reputation on the line; if we teach someone a Direct-Response Marketing strategy, and it doesn't work, they know it doesn't work. Now, we could be like those ad agencies and take their money and say, "Yeah, we'll do some advertising for you," but it's never quantified, and we just mail some letters that tell people where that business is and try to get them to come into the store. But unless it's Direct-Response-driven, there's no way for them to know whether we're worth the money they're spending. **With Direct-Response Marketing, we can tell directly whether that company is making money with the**

strategies we're teaching them.

I assure you, once someone starts using Direct-Response, they'll start to wonder how they ever did without it. Because again, most people who own their own businesses are very good at what they do, but they're not so good at marketing or doing all the little things it takes to keep a business together. Let me tell you a story that Chris Lakey recently told me. It's funny, and while this isn't necessarily a marketing strategy, I think it illustrates the point. Chris's lawnmower broke, and he has a lot of land to mow — he lives on 14 acres of land. So he started paying someone else to mow his yard. Now, ironically, Chris has less and less incentive to want to fix his mower, because he doesn't have to spend time mowing. The other guy just does it for him! That guy has mowed several times now, and originally he told Chris that he would let him know what he'd charge after he mowed it and knew how long it took him. Chris had a ballpark estimate, but wasn't sure exactly how much the guy would charge. But the guy never did get back to Chris for payment like he said he would.

Well, Chris wanted to pay him immediately, so after a few mowings, he called the man up and asked, "Are you going to give me a bill? I need to pay you. What do I owe you?" The other guy said, "Well, I've got notes. I've got it written down, but you're okay. I know that you're going to pay me. I'm not worried about it." And so Chris said, "All right, I just want to make sure you know I'm not trying to stiff you. I just haven't got a bill from you. I need to know how much to pay you." The other guy says, "Yep, that's true."

So a few more weeks pass, and Chris still hasn't seen a bill from the guy — and yet he's coming out and mowing every week or so, because it's a wet spring, and the grass is really growing. Chris sees him coming or going occasionally, or his wife tells him, "Yeah, he was out here mowing today and he didn't leave an invoice, so I didn't know how much to pay him." So Chris picked up the phone and called him again, and the guy admits, "All right, well, here's the truth. **I'm a really good lawnmower, but I'm not such a good bookkeeper!** I've got all my notes, I just haven't figured it all out and gotten you a bill yet. But don't worry about it — it's me, not you." Finally, after the fifth or sixth time he mowed, he finally left an invoice — Chris had accumulated quite a bill!

That's typical of the problem with local business owners. They're good at what they do. He's a good lawnmower; Chris is pleased with him. And yet he's not such a good bookkeeper. He tells Chris he's busy, and yes, his schedule is pretty tight — he's got a lot of referral business. In this case, his problem is not marketing, it's administrative. But the point is the same: he's a good mower, but not such a good bookkeeper. **There are a lot of people with small service businesses who are really good at doing what they do, but again, most of them are *pathetic* at marketing.** Some of them are doing okay because they've got friends; their business is referral-based. But they *could* enhance their business! The lawnmower man Chris uses has a busy schedule, but if he would advertise, he could actually start a fleet and have another person or two mowing for him. He could hire a whole team of people. Even though some of those kinds of businesses think they're limited by the number of hours that they have themselves, if they would expand their thinking and bring in as much business as possible, they could hire somebody else they could pay a little bit less to mow, and start making money off of their efforts as well.

Most small businesses are struggling with their marketing, and some of them aren't good at referrals either. You could talk to them, and they'll tell you their business is suffering, the economy is down, or whatever. **They make all kinds of excuses — but the reality is that they just don't know how to market.**

Too often, these people are trying to wear all the hats in their company all at the same time — and usually the hat that suffers is the one they know the least about, and that's how to market and bring in new customers.

If you own a home, you've probably been approached by people who want you to buy replacement windows, siding, soffits, and such. And they always come walking up to your front door, don't they? They don't have a clue what they're doing. You could point to your window and say, "Don't you see these double-pane, argon-glass, high efficiency windows here? I don't need new windows. Why are you talking to *me*?" And they'll say, "Well, it's my job. I have to give you this flyer. Do you want any soffits or do you need any siding?" It doesn't matter if you live in a brick home, they offer you siding.

And sure, right now is a good time for them, because the Federal government is giving you a $1,500 tax credit to go green in your house — and that includes high efficiency windows, siding, and all the stuff they sell. So there's an incentive there. Now, I don't need any of that stuff, but I look at the flyers that they're using. Not only do their salespeople not have a clue, their flyers are crap. Their headlines are weak; they're not consumer-driven and don't get anybody's attention. The flyer they're handing out has been copied 9,000 times. It's horrible. When Chris Hollinger gets a flyer like this he asks the salesman, "Are you the #1 salesman in your company?" And they always say, "No." Chris says, "Do you want to be?" and of course they say, "Yes." Chris tells them, "Well, here's my number. Give me a call when your feet get tired."

And you know what? Chris has *never* gotten a call back from any of those salesmen, and he has a perfect plan for them that uses Direct-Response Marketing. It's ready to go, ready to generate highly qualified leads that could make them the superstar in their company. They just have to pay him for the leads. But none of them ever, ever calls him! They need to, but they won't.

Their advertising is horrendous. You've seen it in your own mailbox or on your door, when you get copies of flyers that are all wore out and horrible looking. Maybe the headline was good at one time, but now it's so faded you can't even tell what it is. But still, someone's making money on them. **Well, if they can make money on crap marketing, imagine how interested they are when we show them the good stuff!** Telling someone like this, "Hey, I can help you make more money" is music to their ears. It's something they really want.

How would I use Direct-Response in a situation like this? Let's look at replacement windows, for example. I can go get a list of addresses in a specific area of town. Then I can write up a really nice-looking mailing piece that goes out directly to each person. Heck, I can even customize it with that person's name! And I can tell them, "Look, by replacing your windows today you're going to get a $1,500 income tax break next year." That's a nice little headline right there. And what happens instead of having to go out there beating the pavement, trying to sell windows? I get someone to raise their hand and say, "T.J, I want to know more." I hardly know anything about replacement windows — but I do know how to get someone to raise their hand and ask for more information. At that point, I've got someone who wants someone to come out there, measure their windows, tell them about the windows on offer, and give them a quote.

I could call one of these siding and window-replacement companies and say, "Look, how much is a lead like that worth to you? Is it worth $50? What's the average sale you're going to make? Is it going to be $5,000? Is it going to be $10,000? Is it going to be $20,000?" I know for a fact that one of Chris Hollinger's neighbors spent over *$28,000* on siding and replacement windows. So would one of those companies want to pay me $100 or $200 for a highly qualified lead? And when they converted one of those leads into a good sale, would they come back to me and want more leads? Sure they would. **That's the power of Direct-Response, a power that so many businesses aren't using right now.** They're leaving money on the money tree, just waiting to be plucked, because they're not using the right advertising and marketing.

Another reason why this idea is so effective is because it features a benefit. For example, most people don't really want replacement windows — they've already got windows, so why do they need new ones? But there's a benefit if they get new windows: in addition to saving 30% or more on heating and cooling, they can save $1,500 on their taxes. That's what they really want.

Chris Hollinger's brother actually does replacement windows. He has this special camera now; he can take a picture of your house and show you exactly where the heat or the cool air is escaping. **Now imagine getting a mailer, and you see a picture of *your* house, and it shows all the cool air that's coming out around this specific window.** A picture is worth a thousand words! Chris's brother is all excited about his camera, so he and Chris are going to put it to work with some good marketing and advertising — and people are going to line up, and he's going to make a fortune selling windows.

Hey, the best marketers always win. Sometimes they even win with inferior products and services. In a perfect world, only the companies that delivered the very best products and services would be the ones that were the real winners — but in the world that we actually live in, the best marketers are at the top. The ideal, of course, is to be an excellent marketer who delivers top-quality products and services.

The second market we serve consists of all the people

who've thought about starting a home-based business, or a business of their own, but they just haven't made the plunge yet. We can have no real way of knowing how big that market is, but it certainly numbers in the tens of millions. I think it's safe to say that, at one time or another, almost everyone has thought about starting their own business. Back in the 1850s, Ralph Waldo Emerson said, "America is another name for Opportunity." It's part of the American Dream. Most people hate their jobs, just like I hated mine back in the mid-1980s. They want to do something different. They want a piece of the American Pie. They want part of that American Dream.

Now, how is this timely? Because there are an estimated *76 million people* who are commonly referred to as "Baby Boomers." I'm one, and so is my wife and many of our friends. If you're not a Baby Boomer, your parents probably are. We're the people who were born between the years 1946 to 1964 — and we ain't getting any younger. The older a person gets (and I'm speaking from some experience here, because I'm turning 50 this year), the more they start thinking about things they don't normally think about. The older you get, the more that window of business opportunity closes. **People are getting serious about making a lot of money, where before they really weren't that serious.** That's part of the timing aspect of CLUB-20 International.

Another part of the timing aspect is the fact that, as people reach that golden age of retirement, they find out one of two things. Either they don't have enough money at the end of the month and need to make more, so they're going to be attracted to having a home-based business — or they find retirement isn't all it's cracked up to be. As I mentioned in Part One of this book, I watched my dad and stepdad both retire. Both men looked forward to it; my dad even counted down the days till he could retire. But when both men retired; the phone quit ringing; there was no place to go all day; they sort of got out of the flow of life — and it turned out to be a very bad experience for both of them.

A lot of people are like that. I know a guy who had a high-level government job that let him retire early. He counted down the last three years, marking out each day on the calendar with an "X," just like prisoners supposedly do. He hated his job. All he was going to do afterward was play golf every day, and he wasn't even 60 yet. He had this elaborate fantasy world worked out in his head. Well, within nine months after he retired, he had gained 40 or 50 pounds; he was watching TV all the time and sitting around on the couch too much; and he'd started feeling sluggish and unproductive. The reason I knew him was because I offered him a job, and he started working for us. The weight came off. He became productive again, and now he has his own business. I haven't seen him for a year because of that.

You see, a lot of people are going to find that retirement isn't all it's cracked up to be. We Baby Boomers are getting closer to that age, and CLUB-20 International has products and services that are specifically aimed at helping them make more money when they do, in fact, start their businesses. So, with our products and services, we solve an existing problem that's part of a long-term trend.

One of the things that people who near retirement age are looking forward to the most is having free time. They're looking forward to the more sedentary life. And some of them do retire and enjoy just sitting around doing nothing, but many end up going back into the work force, or doing something else, because they have *too much* free time. Many of those people have dreamed of being in business for themselves for many years, maybe their entire lives, but never were able to do it. There was always something stopping them. Well, now that they're retired, they've got the time, and they've probably got their life savings sitting in the bank. They've worked toward retirement; they've built a nest egg; and they want to do something with it, so a lot of them turn to business. Some will start franchises; some will set up local service businesses that help people and help them stay active — **and some of them will look for opportunities like CLUB-20, where they have a chance to live a relaxed and enjoyable lifestyle, but still be productive and earn a great income while keeping their minds sharp.** The retiring Baby Boomers represent a huge, untapped marketplace that's going to grow substantially over the coming years.

But then there's the broader class of people in the opportunity market, too. These are people who've been looking for some fantastic opportunity, and they may not be retirement age. These people range anywhere from 18 to 80, sometimes younger, sometimes older. They come from all kinds of demographic groups: men, women, people who live on the East Coast, the West Coast, people from other countries. There is really no one demographic to that defines them. The only thing that counts is that they're looking for some opportunity like CLUB-20 International. **This is a huge group, and it's growing as people lose their jobs in this moribund economy.** Recently, it seems like the marketplace has been losing about half a million jobs a month. Who knows how long that trend will continue? If you're reading this at home sometime well beyond 2009, perhaps — hopefully — we've bucked that trend, and you're enjoying good economic times. It's hard to say exactly what to expect. But I do know that right now, as people lose their jobs, a lot of them are looking for a side business they can start. **We think that CLUB-20 International gives them exactly the advantages they're looking for.**

So it's timely — to Baby Boomers who are nearing retirement and to the millions of people that are struggling in this economy, looking for a way to supplement their income, because they've either lost a job or they're afraid of losing a job. A significant percentage of those people will be looking for opportunities.

I really do think that America still stands for opportunity. This is truer now than it was back in the 1850s. **What better time to be part of this industry than right now, when millions of people are starting new businesses?** Having said that, there are Baby Boomers who created markets all through their life cycle; and of course, the group as a whole has created or bolstered whole companies and industries as they've matured and aged. Many of those industries and companies are just going to grow as they age further and retire.

And to add to that big group of people, there are plenty of young people today who aren't buying into the typical "go to school, get your education, get a good job and stay with that job for 40 years, and then retire" mindset. They're not buying into that, as if it were even possible now. Some of that is symptomatic of an "I want it all now" mentality, which has its downside, but that's what a lot of the young people want nowadays. They don't want to have to wait to be able to afford to buy their own homes; they don't want to have to wait to be able to afford to buy that car they want. So what are they doing? **They're not going out and getting an entry-level position with some company, or latching onto any of the other more traditional vehicles for their careers.** They're looking for a home-based business opportunity that can put the money in their pockets right away, money that they really want and need. And they're finding it in technology. They're finding it in opportunities. It's a growth industry. **Even in a down economy like today's, there are people making lots of money in the home-based business industry, and CLUB-20 is exactly what they're looking for.**

So when we're talking about timing and positioning, we're

positioning ourselves at the right time to be able to capitalize on a lot of demographics. The common denominator isn't age or gender; it's not any of the traditional demographic categories. If you want to zoom in on it like that, it's just a dollar sign. That's what people want and need. Some of them need it right now just to survive in our economy.

What people really want is what we're giving them with CLUB-20. That $60,000 in 90 days... that's what they want! **They want fast cash, and that's what our system is designed to give them.** Part of what makes it timely is the fact that it's brand new. These days, more than ever before, people are addicted to anything that's new. In the business opportunity market, people are always looking for something new, something different, so that's what we offer with CLUB-20 International.

I've spent a lot of time on the first reason here, because it's part of the foundation of our philosophy. So is the SECOND REASON that CLUB-20 has the potential to make you rich: **In many business opportunities, many people are making huge mistakes — and they're getting rich in spite of them.**

There's a famous business consultant named Jay Abraham who works out of Los Angeles. He bills himself as the world's most expensive consultant. I think, nowadays, he tells people that he charges $5,000 an hour. I've never paid him $5,000 an hour, and I don't know of anybody personally who has. But I imagine he's probably had a few takers. He's a pretty famous guy. I've listened to hours and hours of him on seminar tapes that I've bought — he's a pretty smart guy, too. One of the things that Jay says is this: **"The real secret to wealth is to find average people who are making money in spite of the fact that they're making some serious mistakes."** When you find that situation, lock into it, because you can make a fortune. First of all, the simple fact that they're average means that if they can do it, **anybody can do it.** And second, if they're making money in spite of mistakes, then all you have to do is come along, **correct those mistakes,** and rake it in. That's really the whole formula. That's as easy as it is.

The reason we were so attracted to the company in Panama City that we based our comp plan on is simple: because such *very* average people were making money with it. A lot of these people had never made any substantial amounts of money in their lives, but now they were knocking down $20,000-$50,000 a month just working out of their homes. **And yet, they were making three mistakes that we noticed right away.**

First, they were trying to sell too much, too fast. It was like a guy going to a singles function and asking every woman he saw to marry him. That's a bad approach — it's trying to do too much, too fast. First you've got to take them out to a movie and dinner, romance them a little bit, and prove to them that you're a good person. After about six months of dating, *then* you ask them for their hand in marriage. Well, these people were making good money, but they were telling too much too fast. They were putting their whole thing out there from the outset. But you can't just reveal everything all at once; marketing is a process. You have to give it to people at their own pace.

The second mistake was: they were all doing personal selling — selling to people in person and on the phone. That's a big mistake because, first of all, the average person doesn't want to sell anything, so that leaves a lot of the market out. I don't blame them; I don't want to do personal selling either. There are smarter ways to make money than to get on the phone or talk to people face-to-face. **Part of what Direct-Response Marketing is all about is a smarter way to sell things.**

The third thing they were doing wrong was: they had no marketing system in place. They were having month-to-month cycles of feast or famine. Their businesses were like roller coasters when it came to income. We have friends who are smart marketers, but they have no marketing systems built into their businesses — and so one month they're making a lot of money, two months later they're not even able to pay their bills.

When we got involved with that program out of Panama City, we fixed those problems. Within a relatively short period of time, we brought in over a million dollars. We're no longer involved with that program, but **we've taken the best parts of it and integrated it into CLUB-20 International.** Part of our way of correcting the first problem, where most people are trying to sell too much too fast, is to give them a 472-page book that's chockfull of good value. They can go on Amazon.com and pay $19.95 for this book — or, they can get it for just $5 shipping and handling to prove that they're serious. So we're not trying to do too much too fast. We're giving them something of real value, and we're making a good impression — just like a man would try to do on his first date.

And here's the thing: as many marketers quickly learn, you don't have to be perfect — you just have to be good enough. There are many businesses out there that are just that. **I think one of our strengths at M.O.R.E., Inc. is that we can identify the mistakes other marketers are making, correct those mistakes, and it automatically differentiates us in the market.** We come in with a better plan of attack and a better product overall that grabs people's attention, because it rises above those obvious problems no one else was fixing. It's a unique way to position yourself, right from the get-go.

When some of us marketers look back at what we were doing when we started out, we have to ask ourselves, "Man, how did I put food on the table?" Because we were learning as we went — and that's fine, because it's a great way to get started. We look back and see that we were good enough at the time to survive, because **good enough really is good enough.** But we learn from that how to become great. And one of the things you ask yourself when you're evaluating opportunities is, "What mistakes are being made by this particular company, and how can they be improved upon?" This is especially something you should look at when dealing with an MLM or Network Marketing firm. What's strong about their marketing? What's weak about it?

Nine times out of 10, a Network Marketing company's only system is this: the warm market. Chris Hollinger calls them "warm market mongers." With most Network Marketing companies, that's their whole gig. They want you to sell to your friends and family, because they know the average person can get 4-6 sales that way. After that, they can't make any more sales; there's no system there. The next thing they tell you is, "Invite people to conference calls." And don't get me wrong — this whole warm market approach has built billion-dollar industries. It's especially common in the insurance field, where you hire a new agent and teach him to sell life insurance, so he can sell so many policies to his friends and family. But after that, what system do they have in place? Are you charismatic enough to continue that gig and keep making sales? Or are you informed enough to be able to create your own system to get people to raise their hand and say, "Yes, I want to talk to you about life insurance." It's a system that's proven successful for the people that are starting the companies, and I don't want to criticize them too harshly, because I know people who have become successful that way.

But after your warm market, what's the average guy starting a new home-based business going to do? Pretty soon you end up in **that proverbial NFL Club—"no friends left"**— because you've hit them up over and over again for all these opportunities. You get their voice mail when you call, and when you go over there, even though their cars are in the driveway, for some reason it seems like they're not home! They don't want to talk to you anymore. We want to get people beyond their warm market by developing a system that's Direct-Mail-driven and doesn't require you to talk to your friends and family. Now, of course, if you have a friend or a family member who's looking for a good opportunity, welcome them into CLUB-20. It's not about avoiding your friends and family; **it's just about only targeting the people who are most interested.**

We want to get people beyond their warm market, out where they're attracting people who are specifically interested in making money, and we do that through things like the free book. You can create classified ads, postcards or whatever to advertise and get people to say they're interested. From that, you're working with a smaller group of prospects who've expressed an interest in what you have and are most likely to buy from you. **It's much better to work with a small group of qualified prospects than a bigger group of people who don't know you and have no connection to you.** Once they've requested information, you're in a position of power. That's what a good system can do for you!

The joke about most MLM companies is that they really don't know anything about marketing. The more you understand about marketing, the more you'll know that that's true. Their whole concept of marketing is selling to friends and family. That *is* one aspect of marketing, but not a very long-term, attractive one. And then too, with most opportunities, the only people who ever make any substantial amounts of money are those who have gone through a lot of training and have a lot of experience. They're heavy hitters. They have special skills and abilities. Well, part of our secret is that our parent company has been researching business opportunities for 20 years now. Over 20 years! **We home in on deals where the participants are**

average and are making a lot of money.

So when examining a new opportunity, focus on the marketing system. What is it, and how does it work? Is it based on Direct-Response? Is it based on online marketing? How do you get people to basically raise their hand and say, "Yes, I want to know more"? Once they've raised their hands, are there steps in place to get them to say yes to an entry-level price point, and then say yes to a higher-level price point, and then on from there? Is there infrastructure in place to facilitate additional sales? **The system is critical.** Without it, you're going to have a great idea and spike in sales one month, but you're going to fall off the next, and you're going to have to constantly re-invent yourself. **A system keeps you more on an even keel, and keeps those leads and money coming in.**

I've talked about how marketing is kind of like dating — you have to build up the relationship before you pop the big question. In fact, about 10 years ago we actually created a program where we compared dating and marketing, and talked about how you can use some of the psychological aspects of marketing to attract a partner. We even had a dating expert on the program with us — but mostly, we were talking about marketing and how you don't want to go over the top when you're trying to date somebody. You don't come right out the first time you meet somebody and say, "I want to marry you!" You date them for a while, you get them to warm up to you first, and *then* you pop the question.

Our book *$60,000 in 90 Days* is the foundation of our CLUB-20 "dating system." **The book introduces people to opportunity and, specifically, to the chance to make money with our Wealth Explosion Seminar** — not only by attending that event and getting all the benefits and secrets we're going to share over those three days, but also by selling the tickets to that event in such a way that you can make $60,000 in 90 days using our automated system. **The book helps you ease people into buying the main event.**

Our Wealth Explosion Seminar is an expensive seminar. It's priced comparably to similar events, but it's not what I would call a "budget" event. So you wouldn't want to just approach someone and say, "Hey, would you like to come to my event? It costs several thousand dollars to buy a ticket, but I think you'd benefit." You'd want to sneak it up on them a little. You'd want to warm them up to the idea of who you are. You'd want to first tell them your story and why they should listen to you, and then you'd want to tell them about the opportunity — and then you'd get specific later. **You do that through lead generation** — through, first of all, generating a prospect that's interested in making money. And then. you tell them about the free book. You tell them that the book is theirs; all they have to do is pay $5, which doesn't even cover the cost of shipping and handling to get the product out to them. Actually, the book costs almost five bucks just to print and then, of course, there is shipping on top of that. We ask for $5 just to help prove they're serious, and to help offset the cost of getting the package out to them. What it amounts to is a baby step for them.

You know they're interested in making money, because you're advertising in the right kinds of places to attract those people. You're either renting a mailing list containing the names of opportunity seekers, or you're running an ad in a publication like *Home Business Magazine* that's targeting people who are looking for businesses to get started with. So you're reaching the right person — and you tell the story slowly. You offer them a free book that explains things, and then the book gives them a few more details. **When they get the book, they also get a call from one of our sales reps, asking if they have any questions about the book or about the opportunity.** We slowly unveil that to them, and then we start putting more and more pressure on them. The more they know, the more we demand a decision from them: "Are you in, or are you out?"

That's something that a lot of people have difficulty doing, and it's why they run into problems in any home-based business. They're very uncomfortable asking for the money. **A good Direct-Response Marketing piece asks for the money for you, and it's out there working all the time.** Someone has to pick it up and read it; you're not on the phone trying to twist somebody's arm and convince them they need to get into something. **Our system asks for the money multiple times.** You have to have that; you can't be afraid to ask for the money. You need to make sure you're comfortable giving them the value they need to justify that expense. That all comes from building an irresistible offer. **We have a complete system that does this for you; this is our strength and our power.**

The <u>THIRD</u> <u>REASON</u> CLUB-20 International has the potential to make you rich is that **you can get paid huge sums of cash that comes to you super-fast.**

Remember, we're the exact opposite of most MLM companies. They pay small commissions spread out over large groups of distributors. Now, there are some good companies out there; I don't want you to think that just because I'm slamming MLM, that means that I'm down on the whole industry. In fact, I'm very excited about two traditional MLM companies that we're behind right now. We're using our nontraditional forms of marketing to promote those companies; and yet we know that it's going to be a 3-5 year commitment on our part before any substantial money is made. Even with our marketing, it takes time to sign up hundreds or thousands of other distributors. I think it's ironic that MLM has gotten categorized as a "get rich quick" industry when, in fact, it really does take time. *All* businesses tend to take time. The U. S. Department of Commerce says it takes 2-5 years before you can expect to make a profit in most businesses.

CLUB-20 is all about paying the most money quickly, right up front. With our Wealth Explosion Seminar, we're paying $1,000 commission checks — and we're paying those checks super-fast. Most MLM companies count on something that's called "breakage." In traditional Network Marketing, you have a matrix of some kind, and the company pays out a maximum of, say, 70-80% of what their distributors bring in. But no one ever completely maxes out the comp plan. Most people end up bringing in a couple of others; if the program pays over five levels, they only fill one or two, so there are a bunch of levels uncompleted. Well, even if the maximum payout is 75%, the average distributor maybe only ends up receiving about 40%. That's considered breakage. The company *could,* in theory, pay out a maximum of 75%, but because of breakage, they pay an average of 40%. They're okay with that, because they're making more money.

What companies usually do is throw in a lot of special stuff like bonuses, unique compensations, all kinds of levels, special overrides and extra commissions, and, when they add all those things up, they're able to say they pay out a big number like 75-80%. **But in reality, most people never qualify for those things.** Only the heavy hitters earn those, and yes, some people do make it that far. But most people have no idea or understanding about breakage, and they *never* earn that maximum. They haven't done enough to bring in enough volume, to bring in enough people, make enough sales, or whatever else they have to do to fully max it out. Before you can make any substantial amounts of money with most MLM companies, you have to have hundreds or thousands of people in your downline. Most people never get hundreds or thousands of people in their downline, do they? And so the companies never have to pay out much.

But with CLUB-20 International, only two people get paid as part of our compensation plan. I realize that doesn't seem all that exciting at first, because in traditional MLM, when only two people get paid, that doesn't result in a lot of money. **And yet our two levels are surprisingly profitable.** By using our marketing system to bring in an average of just one new person every week, who then turns around and also decides to become a distributor, within a year **you could potentially make $180,000 a month.** And that's an example only. It's atypical. **It's not a promise or guarantee.** And yet, it's proof that with a compensation plan that pays large commissions to small groups of distributors, it is quite possible to make tens of thousands of dollars a month. We're paying people money right away, not after 3-5 years of hard work. **People need money, and they need it now — and that's what CLUB-20 is all about.**

We're much more like a distributorship on steroids, a distributorship that's amplified, rather than a standard MLM company. Part of the challenge of MLM is that just because you build a downline of hundreds or thousands of people, that doesn't mean those people are going to stay in. Huge numbers of people drop out constantly in MLM. **But here's our idea: a happy, motivated distributor who's making good money doesn't drop out.** So our goal is to get people making big money quickly, and then have them keep making big money, so they'll stay in long-term.

You know, this whole concept of breakage is the dirty little secret of Network Marketing. It really is, because they know that they can dangle this huge number in front of folks and know, going in, that the vast majority of people will never attain it. I've been to Network Marketing Company events all over the country where they bring up the bigwigs of the company — the guys who are doing phenomenally well — and invariably, regardless of their particular compensation plan, they'll say

CHAPTER SIX: The First Five Reasons

something like this: "At first the checks were very small. But NOW I'm making..." and they'll show you this humongous number as a carrot. Now, which compensation plan would you rather be part of? **One that, from the very beginning, gives you some very nice checks, or one that's going to trickle in for starters and then *maybe* you'll get big enough to get to the bigger levels?** That's a question that you need to ask yourself. With the vast majority of Network Marketing companies, there's no mechanism that's going to put a lot of money in your pocket quickly — unless you're a marketer who can dump thousands of people into something overnight.

The <u>FOURTH</u> <u>REASON</u> why CLUB-20 International has the power to make you rich is the fact that **we're paying people giant sums of residual income every single month**.

We're giving people the ability to do something once and get paid over and over again. That's what residual income is all about. There are basically three ways to get paid in anything. There's the first way, which is how most people make their money: **you work an hour, you get paid an hour.** We don't think that's a very good plan; there are better ways to make money. Even if you're a brain surgeon, and you're making hundreds or thousands of dollars an hour, you can still only work so many hours a day. You can still get sick sometimes, or not be able to work, or whatever. So the first way of making money is not the best way if you want to get rich. **The second way to make money is from the sale of a product or service.** The amount of money you're earning has nothing to do with the amount of time that you're putting into it, but has to do with the commissions or the profits you're making from selling the product or service.

The third way of making money is more passive. In the case of CLUB-20 International, you're getting paid on the products or services that our marketing system sells for you.

And then on top of that, you're also getting paid for the products and services that our marketing system sells for the people we put into your team. This method of making residual income is part of the whole secret behind our "$60,000 in 90 Days" concept; it's the leverage principle. **So you have a lot of things that are making money for you other than the amount of time that you put into it.**

All the world's richest people make money using the second or third methods — by selling products or services, or earning residual income. **You've especially got to find a way to get some passive, residual income coming in your life.** Every Fortune 500 company, every Fortune 1000 company, all have residual income built into their business models. So working an hour and getting paid for that hour's worth of work isn't a good strategy. **Residual income is also good, because you've got to have things that are making money for you automatically.** You need money that just keeps coming in on a consistent, regular basis, because your bills come in every month on a consistent, regular basis, don't they? You've got to have something to counter that. **CLUB-20 gives you that advantage.**

A lot of people have a hard time getting to the point to where they're actually generating residual income every month, based on something that they've done months, or even years, prior. It takes a mindset change, because there are so many people out there who were trained to work for that hourly wage and put in their 40 hours a week, with the weekends off. It takes a new way of thinking to get to the point where you're willing to invest time now so that you can get paid later — to do things once and get paid again, or to involve yourself with something where you get paid based on other people's time and people's money. But it's worth it, **because residual income allows you to actually develop a lifestyle that you really want.** Obviously, a lot of people have their dreams about the lifestyle they would like. It's always out there somewhere, but getting it really boils down to the ability to produce income that comes in month after month.

To do that, you need to look at an opportunity's comp plan to determine whether you can do something once and get paid repeatedly. Can you make money off of other people's efforts, because it's in your mutual best interest? I think that's a very important point here. *Is* it in their best interest to work hard for you? When they earn money, does it put money in your pocket? **If those elements are there, then you've got something that's going to build residual income, because nobody can own or stockpile time.** Once it's gone, it's gone, and you only have so much of it. So can you position yourself and build the types of residual mechanisms you need to succeed? One of those is a dynamic compensation plan that pays you a bunch up front and then keeps paying you over and over. But it has to be more than just words and numbers on paper. **There has to be infrastructure and incentives to make it happen.** If not, it fizzles and dies. Now, is there a limit to how long you'll get paid for the work of the people in your team, that second level of your downline? Not at all. **You get paid for everyone forever, as long as they keep bringing in the money.** When they earn their $1,000, you earn an identical amount. If you bring in a heavy hitter, somebody who makes a hundred sales a month, then you're going to get $100,000 a month just from their efforts.

And another point: **that $1,000 commission is only for our flagship product, our Wealth Explosion Seminar. We have coaching program packages available, and in the future through CLUB-20, we expect to offer a number of other products and services.** The compensation plan will always operate the same basic way; so that if your team member sells a product, whatever it is, they'll earn a commission, and you'll earn a matching one. If that happens to be a product with a $500 commission, they get paid $500, and you'd get paid $500 for bringing them in. So that model holds true regardless of what's sold.

We like to talk a lot about $60,000 in 90 days, because that's the name of our book; and it's a good example. A lot of our clients talk about wanting to make millions of dollars. That's great, but the reality of it is that *one* sale would probably help you a lot. Think about the things you spend money on each month. A thousand dollars makes most people's mortgage payment. Just one commission a month would probably pay for just about any car you wanted. Most of us deal with monthly payments; that's how we equate things. When we're thinking about bills, we have our monthly payments for this and for that. Of course, you can't go buy a car outright for $1,000, and you can't buy a house for $1,000. But it would make your monthly payment, wouldn't it? **Just one sale a month using our automated system would provide a lot of relief for you.** And don't forget the fact that each time you do that, that's another person we can invite to become a member of your team, so you can make $1,000 every time *they* make a sale. Over the course of a year, you'd have 12 people. If those people were also advertising and making one sale a month, that would be $12,000 a month. So the math adds up fairly quickly!

If you make just three sales a month, you could have a nice car, a nice house, some vacation money. **It doesn't take big numbers to make a lot of money and provide a lot of relief for you and your family.** That's one thing we want to point out, because we talk a lot about big numbers — and you *can* make huge amounts of money. We like to advertise the number $60,000 in 90 days. Well, we did better than that when we started advertising this and testing our theory. The one thing we had going for us, of course, is that we had a mailing list to offer it to immediately, so we didn't have to build a list. But that's all we had going for us. **The sales team that made those sales for us is the same team that will be working for you. The same system is in place.** Now, the book was still being written when we first did our tests, so we didn't even have that to offer! We gave away a Special Report. So you actually have a little bit of an advantage, because you're giving away something of real value.

We talk about these big numbers a lot, because they're potentially possible... and a lot of people get excited about big numbers. But again, the reality is, **it doesn't take big numbers to make good money for you.** I think most of you probably would agree that just one, two, three, four, or five sales a month would probably change your life. So that's what we're talking about here. **We have big profit potential, but you can make a lot of money with just a few sales.** I've had the chance to speak with opportunity seekers all over the country, and that's one of the things that they've told me over and over again. They don't need $10,000 a month, just enough to pay off the occasional bill. That's where a lot of people are nowadays, and that's why they're looking for a solid, home-based business opportunity that can literally help put them back on the right track financially. A compensation plan like ours is just what they need. **And remember, we've got an automated marketing system that does everything for you.** That system has been perfected over 20 years, in the process of generating over $100 million in sales. And I don't say that to brag on us; I just say it to brag on the system.

That leads directly into the <u>FIFTH</u> <u>REASON</u> CLUB-20 has the power to make you rich: **We do everything for you.**

Now, when you tell people that they can get paid good money, and they don't have to do much to get it, to most of them, it almost sounds like a crime or a scam. They think either there's something illegal or immoral being done, or that it's literally too good to be true. That's because they don't know and understand the business world.

You see, the world's richest people are getting paid on other things besides the amount of time that they put in on something. I read somewhere that it would cost Bill Gates more time and effort than it was worth to him to bend down and pick up a hundred dollar bill that he saw on the ground. That's how much money he makes — some mathematician actually figured that out. I've told you that my best friend has a pest control business. One thing I didn't tell you is that she works at it about 20 minutes a day — and that's being generous. Sure, that 20 minutes a day includes a monthly meeting that she has with her General Manager, where they sit down for 3 or 4 hours every month; but it averages out to about 20 minutes a day. That's a pretty good pay scale for a business that's grossing about a million a year right now. She also has some real estate holdings where money is automatically coming in. She's got a manager who takes care of all of that, too, so she puts in maybe 20 minutes a week on *that* deal.

Rich people are often able to arrange things so that other people take care of everything for them, so they can sit back and make money while others do the work. **Our CLUB-20 system is like that. Our distributors are getting paid for more than the number of hours they put in.** They're leveraging other people's efforts as well as their own, and the rewards are large. Again, when you're evaluating an opportunity, look at that concept of leveraging other people's time and money, and how that relates to putting a residual check in your pocket. A lot of companies can claim, "Okay, you're going to make *this* much money based on other people's efforts." But you want to make sure that those people are incentivized to do that, that there's a reason why that they want to work for you. **If they're making money, you're making money.** So you want to make sure that the real human connection is there. Is it in your downline's best interests to work hard?

That's often not the case, and worse, the companies behind most opportunities have no real incentive to help you. I discussed breakage earlier. Think about the nature of breakage and what it really means. What it comes down to is this: if they help you maximize the compensation plan, they make less money. So they *want* you to fail, or at least not succeed in the maximum way. At best, they want you to make just enough money that you're happy and you stay involved, but they don't want you to make as much money as possible. And they certainly don't want you to max out the compensation plan.

An interesting story of how much the Network Marketing industry really relies on breakage involves a company Chris Hollinger was involved with. It came highly recommended by a friend, so he joined and eventually went to one of the big meetings that they had. When Chris was up on stage presenting, they *specifically* asked him not to mention his style of marketing. That really bugged him, because it was apparently something they didn't really understand. Of, if they did, they didn't like it, and they were really, in Chris's mind, afraid of someone showing a lot of people how to max out the compensation plan. I've mentioned this story before: after Chris got back from the meeting, he had a telephone conversation with one of the company bigwigs who essentially told him, "Now, Chris, if running full-page ads in opportunity magazines and doing Direct-Response mailers really worked, don't you think we'd be doing it?"

Chris replied, "You're missing the whole point. I just dumped over 300 people into your company, using the exact same thing you tell me isn't working." From that point on, he was actively discouraged from using that style of marketing for a variety of reasons, some of which he's never truly understood — other than the fact that **some of the people in charge don't** want the rank-and-file to max out their compensation plan.

But at CLUB-20, we actively want you to leverage the comp plan in a maximal way — because it enriches us when you do! The way our plan is structured, we make an average of $1,000 every time we help you, or one of your team members, make $1,000. We have every incentive to help you make as many sales as possible, because we get paid at the same time we help you get paid. It's simple math: the more sales we can make for you, the more money we'll get. **And you get paid the same amount on your very first sale that you make on your hundredth sale;** no silly matrix or unreachable bonuses.

Now, there *is* one thing you need to do to get the whole system started. Every business needs to be advertised; you can't make big money without advertising. I've already talked to you about how our system works for you. **All you have to do is give away the free book, and to do that, you've got to advertise. But when I say we can do *everything* for you, I'm serious about that.** Not only do we have a system in place for all of the back-end stuff that happens once you bring us a lead, we can even do the front-end advertising for you. We can be your ad agency. I've already discussed our Five Star Mailing System in detail in Part I, but there's more to it than that. You can tell us what advertising you want done, and **we'll have a package available that will do it** — whether you want to advertise on the Internet, or in magazines, or do Direct-Mail. In fact, you can work with the same suppliers that have been the backbone of our success since the early 1990s. I'll go into that more later. But I just wanted to point out that when we say we can do everything for you, we mean it!

I realize that right about now, a skeptical person would be a little upset by the fact that they have to advertise at all. They might think it's all a scheme — despite the fact that we literally do everything else for you. And yet, here's the deal. **We use** what's commonly referred to as a **"two-step marketing approach."** The first step is to do everything possible to attract the largest percentage of the highest qualified prospects. That's the step that you do. The second step is all the follow-up work that we do on our dime. Not your dime, our dime! We're spending our money, because we know it's worth the cost.

Yes, you'll be spending money on the first step, assuming you don't decide to use all free advertising. That first step is getting the book into the hands of the people who are looking for the types of opportunities we provide, the types of products and services we sell. It does cost money. **This is a true partnership between you, our distributors, and us, and because it's a partnership, you're spending money on the first step. But we're spending all of our money on the second step.** And that money includes the fact that your prospects are spending just $5 for the book. The book in quantity orders costs us $6.50 just to print — so we're losing a buck-fifty right there. To ship the book costs another four or five bucks. The Special Report that goes with it costs another couple dollars. Plus, we have to pay for all the follow-up mailings — and postage ain't getting any cheaper! *And* we're also spending money on infrastructure, all of our salespeople, facility costs, and much more. **We're spending our money to help you guys make money.** That's one point I want to drive home, because it's something you don't often see. Most opportunities are happy to ask you to spend your money, but they're not spending any of theirs — and I think that's a joke, really. That's where you're getting scammed. That's not a partnership; a partnership is a give-and-take. A partnership is where the door swings both ways — where you're doing your part, and we're doing ours.

What you're doing offers real value, because you're getting high-qualified prospects to raise their hand. What we're doing is all the things that it takes to make that sale — which is very expensive on our part. **So it *is* a true partnership.** It's not a franchise from a legal perspective, but it's still a franchise in a conceptual way. Consider what a franchise really is: a business that does everything possible to help their franchisees make the largest amount of money, because the parent company — the franchiser — gets a percentage of every dollar the franchisee earns. Like a franchiser, we make our money by helping you make your money. Yes, I know that a lot of business opportunity promoters say the same thing; they even have little bumper stickers with that saying on it. But when you ask them, "How do you really help me?," they start mumbling and giving you a bunch of double-talk, and they really can't give you any solid answers — because the truth is, it's a one-sided deal. What they usually end up saying is, "Well, I'll come over to your house and draw all the circles on the paper and show you and talk to your warm market for you."

The truth is, they're just not interested in you making money. They want to keep that money to themselves and even when they do seem to be honest and in earnest about you profiting, **they don't understand a lot of what marketers like us do.** Case in point: a company we were involved with about five years ago where we generated about a million dollars. The leaders of that company were making good money off us, so they were out to support us. Believe me, they worked with us a lot. We did long conference calls with them, where we were on the phone with them for three hours at a time, and they did all the talking. Chris Lakey and I sat there and pretended to listen, but we were working on our computers at the time and every once in a while we'd say, "Uh huh. Uh huh. Sure."

But I remember very distinctly one time when we were generating thousands of leads by asking people to call in and listen to a recorded message. Our message was 15 minutes long, and the leaders of this company said, "Guys, you're going to

198

have to change that. Nobody's going to sit and listen to a message that's 15 minutes long." And we were nice about it; we bit our tongues and said, "Uh huh. Yes sir. Uh huh." We didn't argue. Somehow, they didn't realize that thousands of people were calling in; thousands of people were listening to the 15-minute message; and thousands of people were then leaving their names and addresses. Generating leads was never our problem, even with a fifteen-minute message. **Our big problem was that we still had trouble converting them.**

While we were on the phone with the bigwigs, we were polite. We were gentlemen. We were good, mature adults; we kept our mouths shut. But immediately after Chris and I got off the call, we said to each other, "We need to make our message longer." They were telling us we needed to make it five minutes long, but they were wrong; to convert folks, we needed a message that was a half-hour or 45 minutes long. Remember, it all goes back to Direct-Response Marketing. A lot of companies just don't understand the type of marketing we do. Making people sit there listening to a message for 15 minutes is actually a part of a system that helps to qualify that prospect. **It all comes down to what hoops you can make that particular prospect jump through to further qualify themselves.** One of the reasons we wanted to do a longer message was that 15 minutes wasn't qualifying the prospect enough. So we thought: "Let's make them listen to us for 45 minutes, and the ones that come out of that pipeline are going to be more qualified — and more apt to say yes — and we're going to be able to spend more money on a more highly qualified group of people." When you do that, you're focusing your advertising and marketing dollars at a group that's more likely to buy.

We think it's a mistake to limit you in the types of marketing you use, so we're not going to do that. After all, you might have a marketing method that works better than ours!

While we recommend that you start out using our system, you don't have to: you're an entrepreneur, and entrepreneurs are all independent-minded people who want to do things their own way. I've mentioned the one distributer we had, years ago, who was doing $5,000,000 a year using our *Dialing for Dollars* system. He was doing *the exact opposite* of most of the things we were telling him to do. He was experimenting with his own ideas. He put his own creativity into it, and he found his own way that worked even better. **So I would encourage you to investigate other options, but start with our stuff, too,** because as the saying goes, **"You've got to know the rules before you can break them."** There are reasons why we do what we do. Now, if you do something that really works, and it's really making you money, maybe you should keep your mouth shut — because chances are, if you tell me about it, I'm going to tell everybody else!

CHAPTER SEVEN:

The Next Five Reasons

The <u>SIXTH</u> <u>REASON</u> our system has the power to make you rich: **We've discovered a whole new way to make money with a proven secret that's already making other people up to $100,000 a month or more.**

There are people out there right now making fortunes this way. This new style of compensation plan that we're working with is being used by various companies, because it's popular at the moment. We see knockoffs all the time; in fact, I recently looked at an opportunity magazine that was full of them. It's becoming a trend to offer comp plans that pay larger commissions to smaller numbers of distributors. Because of that, **people are not only making money fast, they're making *big* money fast!** We've heard stories of people making a couple hundred thousand dollars a month, or even more.

We're unique because we add a system that we've been perfecting for 20 years. It's so simple, it's not even funny. Why more people don't do it is beyond me. **We use two-step lead generation ads to get serious prospective buyers to raise their hands and come to *us* on some type of initial offer.** Sometimes it's free. Sometimes they have to pay a few bucks. On one of our current controls, people have to pay $39.95 on the first step. The second step is heavy follow-up with a long sequential mailing series. Remember how I pointed out that we spend our money to help *you* make money? This sequence we're working on for our flagship event involves 30 different follow-up mailings. Now, that's expensive! Direct-Mail is a very effective way of selling if you do it right, but it's also a very expensive way. So we do more follow-ups than anybody I know of in this market — and I know a lot of people in this market.

Since 2006, we've added a crack team of highly-trained sales professionals who help us follow-up and get sales that we normally don't get through our mail order offers. It's hard to imagine how we actually made it for all those years without having a sales department, because Drew Hanson has built a tremendous one. But we did — and that's testament to the fact that good copy *does* sell. But now we've got this wonderful sales staff, and we're building that department on a regular basis. They go in and make money for us that we wouldn't make without their direct involvement. **And now they're making money for all of our distributors.** If you come on board, they're *your* sales department too.

At the risk of sounding arrogant, **our marketing system is so much better than most of the marketing systems we see other people using. And here's why:** We spend more money than most marketers spend. We do a more effective job of selling than they do, because we're putting our money to good use. We're staying after prospects longer and harder. We're putting more pressure on prospective buyers than most people. This is a lesson that took me years to learn, and every year we get better at it.

One of my early mentors was a guy named Dan Kennedy, whom I have a lot of respect for. I'll never forget one time in 1994 when we were working with Dan. That was when the whole business was still relatively new to me, and I was obsessed with it. I was trying so hard to be a good marketer; it wasn't uncommon for me to work 90-100 hours a week. Think about that. That basically means you get up at 5 AM, you go to bed at 11 PM, and you don't stop working in between. That was my life, and I was obsessed with it. At that time, Dan was working with us on some of our promotions. He helped us produce an infomercial that we tested in 14 cities. We were getting all these leads coming in, but weren't able to make enough sales to cover the cost of our infomercial.

Eileen and I went down to Wichita to see Dan. He was part of a circuit that traveled all over the country, and he was speaking there. We took him out to lunch, and he said, "T.J., tell me what you're doing." So I showed him all the stuff I was doing, and he said, **"You're giving up on your prospects too soon."** Now, we had hundreds and hundreds of leads. And Dan kept saying, "You're not putting enough pressure on them. You're giving up on them too soon. You're not selling them hard enough." I kept saying, "But Dan, look at this. We're doing this and this!" And he was just a jerk about the whole thing. Dan is famous for his "no BS" attitude." He doesn't BS anybody, and won't take it from anybody. I would never say the things he does to people; I want them to like me. I'd never get in their face, like Dan did to me, and say, "Nope, you're giving up."

He just kept driving that home, and I was so angry at him! I was very, very, upset. I felt like grabbing a plate and just throwing it at his head, not that I would ever do that; I think he's a great man, and I respect him. I would never even be insulting to him, so I kept my mouth shut — but inside I was very angry. And I stayed angry! I was resentful. For a number of years I was so resentful, because I was working so hard trying to put this thing together, and for somebody just to say, "Oh, you're giving up on them too soon. You're not selling them hard enough," was like a punch in the gut. **And yet, he was right.**

Nowadays, I've got it! I told you early in this book that I consider myself a very average person. The problem with being an average person is, it takes you longer to understand things. Somebody who's smart can get it just like *that*. Sometimes it takes me months or years to get something; but when I get it, I finally get it! And I get it now! **Today, in 2009, we don't give**

203

up on our prospects too soon. We put a lot of pressure on them. And here's our opinion: **as long as you're selling products and services that deliver on what you say that they do, then you're doing people a disservice by *not* putting all that pressure on them.** So we do put a lot of pressure on people.

There are so many marketers out there working these newfangled comp plans that are trying to do it all over the Internet. And, God love them all, but they're weak marketers — and we can beat them any day of the week. I don't mean to sound arrogant; it's just reality. **We can beat Internet marketers every day of every week because they're so weak.** One of the reasons they're weak is that they're in love with the Internet and want to do everything online. One of the reasons they're in love with the Internet is because they don't have to spend any money on their marketing. They're addicted to that fact. And yet, you *have* to spend money in order to do a complete job of selling and to make money. That's part of what Direct-Response is all about.

Internet marketers are easy to ignore, because it's so easy to blow off your emails. Most people get emails all day long from people trying to sell them stuff. Are you even reading 1/100th of all the emails you get? Nope, most are ignored. **But when you put a big, fat, Direct-Mail package in somebody's mailbox, you've got what we call the "thump" factor going.** Drop it on your table, and it'll make a thump! It's big, because we're doing a complete job of selling. And people pay attention.

With the CLUB-20 follow-up mailings, your prospects are going to experience that thump factor thirty times. Each time they'll get a nice-looking Direct-Mail piece, doing what it's designed to do — to get that new prospect to say yes. That's a hound dog on the scent of a pretty good trail, right there, if you ask me! A hound dog *stays* on the trail. They don't give up. Thirty times we're going to be asking that prospect that you bring in to say "Yes!" Thirty times! So many marketers give up way too soon.

So don't give up on your prospects too fast. Ask yourself: "Where's my price point at, and how much money can I spend to break that sale?" A lot of new marketers get very frustrated very quickly when they don't get the results they thought they should after they've put all this effort into it. They think, "Why aren't people saying yes?" Well, it could be a lot of reasons. It could be your offer. It could be your copy. It could be the fact that they had a fight with their wife or husband the night before. Maybe the dog ate the mail. Maybe that first piece you sent them didn't register for some reason. Maybe it didn't even get there. There are so many different factors in your prospects' lives that you can't control. In any case, the offer didn't get through to them — but then you send another one, or an email, or a phone blast and invite them to a conference call, and they respond. **There are so many different mechanisms at your disposal as a marketer, and to be able to have 30 points of contact built in... that's pretty impressive.** It really is, because it keeps that pressure on, and it overcomes all these things that could be happening with your prospects. Even if he said no to an earlier contact, here comes another one, and maybe he says, "Wow, this guy is serious. Maybe I should think this over."

If I had $1,000 right now for every one of my clients who said these words to me: "Thank you, T. J., for not giving up on me," I'd be buried in money. I've heard that time and time again. They appreciate that we just kept right on after them. And don't forget — in addition to those 30+ pieces of Direct-Mail that **we follow up the initial CLUB-20 contact with, Drew's salespeople are also calling people up constantly.** We're doing a good job of keeping pressure on, mentally and emotionally, by building a good solid offer — so good, so solid, that they just absolutely get to the point to where they can't say no to it.

There's too much value and benefit. The message is clear and easy to understand: "This is everything I'm going to get, and there's the potential, and the great compensation plan, and the great products... and it only costs *this* much?" And in their minds they're like, "Wow!" They can't handle it anymore. It builds pressure on them to where they have no other option than to say yes. That's what we're going for. **So it's not just the quantity of pieces, but also the quality — and the pressure those pieces build in the hearts and the minds of the prospects.**

Obviously, we only send the book out once — unless, of course, someone tells us they want another copy. But beyond that, we send out additional copies of a Special Report that invites them to purchase their own seminar ticket, to become a distributor for our opportunity. **Some of the follow-up pieces that come afterward are sales letters, some are postcards, some are invitations to a conference call —** lots of different things to try to get them to respond. It's not like we send them the same information over and over. We do different things. We try to get them to talk to our salespeople over and over, too, with the constant goal of making it clear, through our constant contact with them, that we're after their business.

This is one benefit of two-step marketing. Because they requested the book from us, we're in the position to approach them as a lead, as a prospect. If we were just to take someone out of the phone book and keep inviting them to come and do business with us, that could be seen as a nuisance. And maybe some people see the mail we continue to send to them as a nuisance. **But the fact is that they requested it from us.** We sent an invitation, they visited our website, they requested the free book — and they understood when they requested the free book that we were going to be inviting them to take advantage of a special opportunity we have for them.

And, the fact is, as I've mentioned previously, we also give those people a **free entry-level position in our opportunity** — we actually send them a start-up package. They're distributors. They could go out and start making sales using our system just because they requested the free book. There's a qualification process all new distributors have to go through, and they have to go through that too. When they talk to our sales reps, we're able to talk to them with more authority about the opportunity they're already involved with.

I've had multiple conversations with our joint venture partners about this, the people who are part of our $100 Million Roundtable. Some of them actually helped us develop this offer. When we tell them how many follow-up packages we send out, they're shocked! They can't believe that we're mailing that many packages to our prospects. **And that tells me that we're doing something right.** When even people who know and understand Direct-Response are shocked at the volume of mail we're sending out, we know we're doing things right. And, of course, we know the costs. We're on top of the profit-and-loss, and we wouldn't do it if it wasn't profitable. Once again, **we're not afraid to spend more money to make money.** After all, people who are timid marketers usually aren't successful. If you're afraid of follow-up, you won't profit. Some people just send out one invitation, and that's it. If people buy, great; if they don't, they move on. And those that make the most money are the ones who relentlessly go after the business.

I've got two personal stories that I think illustrate those points of aggressive persistence and using a system very well. It takes a lot, sometimes, to get through to people and to make that initial sale. My best example: back around Y2K my stepson Chris found the woman of his dreams, and they set their wedding date. Well, Chris was bound and determined that I was going to wear a tuxedo to his wedding. And I told him, "Chris, the only time you're ever going to get a tuxedo on me is the day that I die. Then you can put a tuxedo on me and have an open casket funeral and show everyone, assuming that I don't die in a car wreck or something. But as long as I'm living, as long as there's blood pumping through these veins, I ain't gonna dress up for nobody — because it's just not my thing. I'm not going to do it." I've known Chris since he was seven years old. That's when I met his mom; he was just a little tiny kid. He knew better than to argue with me, and so he kept his mouth shut. But he was determined that I was going to wear a tuxedo to his wedding, and he had nine or ten months to work on me.

Now, Chris knew that I was stubborn and rebellious, so he couldn't just demand that I wear a tuxedo to his wedding, because that wouldn't do any good. If he'd said, "You're going to wear a tuxedo to my wedding!" I would have said, "To hell with that! I'm not either! Watch me! No way!" So he couldn't just come at me like that. He knew that; he's a very smart guy. And so he just kept working at it. For all those months, he just bugged me. He just drove me crazy with this tuxedo thing; he kept trying to sell me on why it was a good idea for me to wear a tuxedo to his wedding, and how I would be the only male family member who wasn't wearing one, and they were going to have all these photographs that were going to last for 30 or 40 years — and I was going to be the dumb fool dressed in a T-shirt and blue jeans when everybody else was dressed in a tuxedo.

He tried to come at me in all these angles. Nothing worked. I wasn't going to wear a tuxedo; no way. And then finally, after about 8 months of working on me, constantly driving me crazy with this tuxedo thing, he finally got me. He caught me on something where I finally said, "Yeah, I guess I could see that was a good idea," and then... BOOM... he pounced on me! To make a long story short, there I am in all the family photographs, alongside all the other male members of the family, all dressed in tuxedos... and I'm dressed in a tuxedo too. I did it, and I'm glad I did it. Really, it would have been wrong for me to be the only family member dressed in a T-shirt and blue jeans when everybody else was dressed up. Anyway, the guy got me — and he got me the way that all good salespeople get their prospects to buy. **He got me through being relentless.**

There's a book by Zig Ziglar's brother, the late Judge Ziglar, called *Timid Salespeople Raise Skinny Kids*. That's a great title. **Timid marketers who give up too soon leave a lot of business on the table, and we don't make that mistake.** So I hope you will remember the tuxedo story. It's one of my favorites. It's a story that illustrates the value of being relentless and not giving up. He was determined that I was going to do this; there was no question in his mind. Although he didn't high pressure me, he *did* bother me, in the same way that a mosquito will bother you. He just wouldn't leave me alone; he just kept bugging me. But finally I did it, and I was glad I did it.

Here's another story I wanted to share. You see, we talk about moneymaking methods as if they're formulas. **If you find out what's making money for one person, and you really study what they're doing and you duplicate it, you'll be able to make as much money as they are, or, in some cases, even more money.** My wife just had her birthday, and she's homebound because she has multiple sclerosis. So she asked me what kind of cake I wanted her to make for me — for *her* birthday. I told her that, because I'm trying to watch my weight, I wanted a carrot cake, because they're supposed to be healthy for you. Well, she'd never made a carrot cake. But she got on the Internet, typed in "carrot cake," and two minutes later she printed out a little recipe. I took it to the store, bought all the stuff she needed, and she followed the recipe and it was very, very good. I think she got about one piece out of it, and I ate the rest! The point is, she made it using a recipe. **Making money is just like a recipe.** If you follow what other people are doing, you can emulate them, just like she followed that recipe. Even somebody like me, who's not a good cook, could do it if I really wanted to put my mind to it and follow a recipe.

The <u>SEVENTH REASON</u> why CLUB-20 has the power to make you rich: **You'll cash-in with a powerful marketing system that none of the people who are already making thousands of dollars a month have or can use.**

There are plenty of companies out there that are doing the types of things we're doing with CLUB-20 right now, particularly in offering this new type of comp plan that pays large commissions to small groups of distributors. But nobody has our 20 years of experience. **Nobody's doing it the way that we are. Everything we have is proprietary based.** It's for our distributors only, and I see it as a real advantage.

Aristotle Onassis, the Greek billionaire shipbuilder, once said that the secret to business is to know something your competitors don't know. And we really *have* perfected some things. Now, our marketing system is basically very simple, but we keep finding ways to improve it. We keep finding ways to make it more effective and to do a better, more complete job of selling.

One example of that is something I've already mentioned a few times, but that I think I should talk about a bit more. **One of the coolest things that we're doing with CLUB-20 International, which no other company that we know of is doing, is making people qualify themselves.** When you're using the marketing system and they send for the free 427-page book, they pay $5, just to prove they're serious and to help offset some of the costs. It's mostly to get a highly-qualified prospect, though. We don't want to waste our time with someone who won't even spend five bucks. We then send them a Report that's really a sales letter. Then we follow-up with them like crazy. But we also give them an entry-level position in our opportunity. **We start them out as a distributor. That's normally a \$97 value; we give it to them absolutely free.**

One of the hardest things you have to do when you want to sell somebody something is to get them interested. People are distracted. We've got so many things to do, and life is so busy these days. All this technology that was supposed to make our lives so much simpler is just making our lives even more complicated, it seems. There's too much going on in our lives. We have information overload. **The degree to which you're able to get people involved will determine your success.** This is one of the reasons why many of these Internet marketers are so weak; they never get people involved. Once you get people involved in something, then they take action and start paying better attention. So we start everybody out as an entry-level distributor, so they can start making money from Day One with our system. They have to go through a qualification period, but they're already a distributor. That's how we get their attention, we get their interest. I know of no other company that does it.

We've done things similar to this before. For example, back in the 1990s, we sold tens of millions of dollars worth of special opportunities we called Master Distributorship Opportunities. One of the ways that we sold those was, first, we made people distributors at low cost or no cost. **Once somebody becomes a distributor, they start paying a little more attention.** Now they're more interested. They get involved in the whole thing and are willing to invest the time necessary to fully go over everything, to read it, to comprehend it, to assimilate it — and that leads to the sale. You only try to sell them a distributorship in the beginning, so you're not trying to do too much too fast. **It's a process.** Remember that. Once they've qualified themselves, you take them to the next level.

A great offer backed by a great marketing system is

absolutely golden — and that's what you have here. You will *not* find another marketer that I know of, or have ever heard of, who's going to have a 30+ point follow-up system in place, unless it's Internet auto-responder crap. But this is Direct-Response, which separates us from the mainstream. And the fact that this has a built-in marketing system that absolutely hammers home the message is icing on the cake. In addition to a flood of Direct-Mail, prospects will get five different calls from us. We're trying to be the competitor that other people look at and say, "My goodness, how in the world are we ever going to beat what those guys are doing?" **What we're willing to do to break a sale sets us above everyone else.**

Don't take this wrong, but we call it the "Chinese Water Torture" form of marketing. That's just a joke, really, but remember what the Chinese water torture is all about. It's just little drops of water — harmless little drops of water on the forehead for a three-day period with no sleep. People just go crazy; they can't take it. But what is it? It's just drops of water. It's harmless, but it wears people down.

You benefit from our automated system, a system we've perfected that no one else has. Other companies have similar opportunities or payment structures, but most also fall into the realm of traditional MLM, where you're left talking to your friends and family. You've got no automated system. **Not only do we have one, but it's based on 20 years of Direct-Response business — and on all the things we've learned about making money in that business.** You benefit from all of those years of research and testing.

That $5 we charge for our book doesn't even cover the cost of shipping, much less printing. It really is a loss for us, yet it gets us a qualified lead. We use our own resources and money to pursue that lead, and **if they don't convert, we lose over a hundred dollars.** If each of those 30 follow-ups cost just three bucks, you're in the $90 range — and that's not even including the initial package. Why do we do it? As I've said, we make an average of $1,000 for every $1,000 we help you make. Simple enough. **We're making a good profit even if we spend all that money to close those leads.** Our numbers show us that we can convert a large enough percentage of those leads to make it worth it for us to spend the money and time following them up. That's the power of our automated system.

Do we do it because we're nice people? No. I think we're nice people, and I hope you think so, too. But that's not why we're able to do it. We'd go out of business, and it would serve nobody if it was a losing financial model for us. So we've built a financial model, and an automated system around that, that lets us make money when we help you profit. That's why we do it, and it ties into our Reason Number Eight.

REASON NUMBER EIGHT: **We have the ultimate reason to do all we can to help you get paid the largest amount of cash in the fastest time.**

Simple enough; it's what I just said. We make an average of $1,000 profit per sale. **We're in there with you. It's a partnership.** We're in an overcrowded market, as you may realize. There are so many different companies selling business and moneymaking opportunities. And one of the popular messages we see over and over again — it's our message too, by the way — is, "We make money by helping you make money." Lots of people say it because it sounds good, and they know that's what people want to hear.

But when you put the opportunity under a magnifying glass and really study what they're doing, and you ask them, "Well, *how* exactly are you going to help me make money?" you don't get any real answers. Even if they do have answers, even if they say, "Hey, we're partners here. We're helping you. You're helping us," press them. Ask, "Yeah, but what *exactly* are you doing for me?" **You'll find they're really not doing much. In other words, they want you to take all the risk.** If you make money, that's great! If you don't make money, that's great, too! They really don't care. They don't have any of their own money invested. Don't you see? To the degree that your partner has invested in it themselves, *that's* the degree that you can really trust the whole thing; that's the degree that it's likely to be on the up-and-up. If somebody is asking you to carry 90% of the load, then how committed are they *really* to helping you? **We're spending a *huge* sum of money in order to help break all of the leads,** where "break" is a term we use for making a sale, converting a prospect to a buyer. We're spending huge amounts of other resources, too, in an attempt to make all of us the largest possible amount of money.

Instead of a win/lose situation, **this is a four-win situation.** You win because you're getting paid $1,000 on every sale our marketing system makes for you. The people we place into your team win, because they get the same advantage. Everybody who's buying the products and services we sell wins, because those things all teach people the same principles and methods we're using to generate our own fortune. And then, last but not least, we win too. We're in it to win it... and we're in it all the way!

Oh, and by the way — we have something new that you're among the first to hear about. **It's called "Prospect Manager Pro Software."** I give Chris Lakey all the credit for that; he's the one who's worked with our developers to put it all together. For the longest time our clients have said, "Is there a way I could stay on top of everything better? Is there a way I can know *exactly* what you're doing for me? Is there a way I can run my whole business better by keeping an eye on everything a little better?" This came out of a desire from our clients to stay on top of it all — not just from the front side where you're bringing in leads, but from a desire to know, "Am I bringing in any leads at all? Is the system working? Are you actually converting leads for me and making sales? Am I earning commissions? What's happening with all the postcards I'm mailing? What's happening with the classifieds I'm running? Is any of that working? How do I know?"

Prospect Manager Pro is a piece of software that runs on the Internet and allows you to track all your prospects, so that you know who they are, and what their status is. We'll be able to keep you informed of whether that prospect just requested the initial package, or whether we're following up with them right now, or even whether you've earned a commission and how much that commission was. **You'll be able to see all of your leads there.** You'll have the mailing addresses of all your prospects. If you wanted to, you could copy that database into your own mailing list manager so you could send them other advertisements. These are your leads, after all; you own them. They're yours to do whatever you want with, though we encourage you to leave them alone while we're working with them. **If you start communicating with them, you could mess up our process and risk losing a sale. But once we've gone through the process, you can do whatever you like in terms of marketing to them.** Let's say you bring in 1,000 leads. Well, obviously not all those prospects will become paying customers. It may be that up to 95-98% of them don't buy; that's just the reality of Direct-Mail. But even if only 2-5% buy, you're still making excellent money.

So what happens with all of those prospects after we're done with them? **Well, they're your leads.** Just because they're out of the sequence and haven't purchased doesn't mean they're a bad customer and will never buy anything. You can mail them an invitation to buy another product or service, you could invite them to join another opportunity, or mail them information on something else — you can do whatever you want with those leads. That's one of the great features about this software: it allows you to see all those leads, so you can get all their information and add them to your own mailing list.

Even if they don't buy, even if someone goes through that whole system and says "No," why not make them another offer? That's one of the most powerful things about the system: **it puts you in a position to really start developing a list of prospects that you can sell to later.** Whether they said yes or no, they've qualified themselves as interested in business opportunities; at one point they raised their hand and said, "Yes, send me the information." They were a qualified home-based business prospect at that point. Just because they said no to CLUB-20 doesn't mean they won't say "Yes" to something else down the road. **CLUB-20's system isn't just a way to leverage our opportunity; it provides you with an infrastructure that can launch you in many different directions.**

It's a pretty powerful system, and it even has a cool map feature that pop ups and shows you where your prospects are physically. Overall, it's a pretty cool piece of software that we're really proud of and excited to introduce. It only cost us a million dollars to build it! This particular fact comes back to that mutual interest factor that I talked about earlier. **It's in our interest to spend this money to follow up with all the prospects. That's one of the things you should look for in any business opportunity: mutual self-interest.** You have to answer that question, because people aren't going to be benevolent for no reason in a business environment. The one thing you should never trust is when somebody says they want to help, just because they like helping people. I know there are some people like that in this world — I know some of them personally — but I think they're few and far between. For the most part, I would be very suspicious of anybody that said that they just want to help you because they like to help. *We* want to help you, because it's good business to do that, and I hope that if I haven't already proven that to you by now I soon will. It's a real partnership. **Again, the door swings both ways.** We help you, but we're also helping ourselves. Self-interest rules the world.

Here's an example that hits home with me. I don't want to embarrass Chris Hollinger, but recently he went through a period in his business where things got a little tough. It happens; we've all had periods like that — many of them, in my case. I wanted to do everything I could to help him, because he's a joint venture partner of mine, and he's a friend. Now, his wife wanted him to go back to teaching school again. She told him, "Chris, we've got to cut this out. I want you to go back to teaching school and get a steady paycheck." And I was saying, "Chris, don't do it! Don't do it!" Part of the reason I was saying that is because I knew that if he was teaching school, he couldn't come help us do our marketing workshops anymore! It was pure self-interest. Do I care about Chris Hollinger? Absolutely. I wanted to help him as a friend — but I also had selfish, self-centered reasons for wanting to help him. Self-interest rules the world! **That's what capitalism is all about: you help me, I'll help you, and together we'll achieve more than either one of us could do on our own.**

The NINTH REASON CLUB-20 has the power to make you rich: **It's designed so that in some cases, it can pay you thousands of dollars within days.**

You can make money within days if you already have a mailing list of people who like you, trust you, and respect you. Remember, I made $10,000 my first week with the company in Panama City. I was able to do that because I already had a base of customers with whom I had excellent relationships. I told them about the opportunity, they got involved, and I made $10,000 in my first week.

CLUB-20 is designed to pay you very quickly, and that's its strength. We're the first company I know of that's ever named the company after its compensation plan — or at least, that's how the name was derived. In our mathematical examples that we use to illustrate the power of our compensation plan, we tell people that all you have to do is use our marketing system to make four sales who then become distributors — people who turn around and do the same thing that you did — and now you'll have four on your first level, and you'll have 16 on your second level, for a total of 20 distributors. If each one of those distributors was to make just one sale, you'd make $20,000. We decided to call the company CLUB-20 just to illustrate the simplicity of that compensation plan.

So many of these MLM plans are anything but simple. In Part I, I told you about the company out of Michigan I was involved in twice. It's an old company that's been around since the 1950s; I can't name it by name, but it starts with an "A." Despite being a member twice, I never understood the comp plan. And it's not that I didn't try, either; I had lots of people trying to explain it to me. They acted like they understood it, but I never did. You've got to be a rocket scientist to figure that thing out.

Our plan is simple. Use our marketing system to make four sales of people who also become distributors. They do the same. You've now got 20 distributors. They make one sale each. If they make one per year, you get $20,000 a year. If they make one each every four months, then you get $80,000 a year. Simple. If they make one sale a month, you get $20,000 a month. Add in our marketing system and Prospect Manager Pro, and you've got a powerful opportunity that's easy to get a handle on. Now, what would it take to earn $20,000 a month in most other companies selling vitamins and juice bottles?

Recently, we were looking at an opportunity, and it seemed

everything was really good about it. Then I started examining the compensation plan a little more closely and worked out that you get a little over $2 for every order. It became clear that it takes a lot of orders to get to any serious commissions. This plan pays up to seven levels. So you can build an army of thousands of distributors, and if you max out the compensation plan, you could make maybe a few thousand dollars a month. Compare that with what you could make if you had thousands of distributors in CLUB-20. **There *is* no comparison.**

Like I said before, most Network Marketing opportunities aren't get-rich-quick. **A lot of them are get-rich-slow (if ever).** Many of them have all kinds of problems. It takes a long time to build a team that can make you the money you can make right away with CLUB-20. Again, CLUB-20 is based on the idea that you just use the automated system to bring in four prospects in Month One. We work with those four people and help them do that same thing in Month Two and in Month Three. By the time you've done that for just three months, we get to the $60,000 in 90 days. But, beyond that, if you just do that on two levels and you get four who each get four, that's 20 people in your team. If all of them are doing the bare minimum and using the system to bring in one sale a month, those 20 people would be making you $20,000 a month.

Now, that's just a mathematical example; **don't take it as a guarantee.** But you can see the math is easy to figure out, and it's easy to see how you can make huge amounts of money. As I said earlier, even if no one ever did that, and you didn't have a team with a bunch of people making sales every month, if you just had one or two team members, each making you one sale a month... well, an extra thousand dollars a month is definitely useful. And it's easily possible here using our automated system combined with a bare minimum amount of work. If you had just brought in one person a month over 12 months, that's $144,000 a year if everybody just does one sale a month. Not too shabby.

So huge amounts of money are possible with just the smallest amount of effort. Of course, some people will make no sales, because they won't do anything. We can't control our distributors; nor would we want to. You're an independent contractor. Some people will choose to do nothing — they'll never advertise; they'll never give away a free book. Unfortunately, that's just the way it is. So not everybody who joins your team will actually do something with it. But when they do a minimum amount of effort — just one sale a month — you can bring in huge amounts of money over time, and that can add up.

Part of the secret to getting rich is to give people what they want, not necessarily what they need. **When it comes to a business opportunity, what people really want boils down to five things:**

1. Fast cash.

2. Easy money.

3. Something that's proven.

4. Something with real wealth-making potential.

5. Something that's going to be a long-term opportunity.

CLUB-20 offers all five of those things. It's definitely evolutionary in every way.

We fell in love with the basic compensation plan we're offering here, because it's something that provides fast cash. You put our marketing system with it, a proven marketing system that's generated tens of millions of dollars in sales for us, and you couple that with the fact that the same people who do all the work for us can now do everything for you, and that

220

makes it easy. **And then you look at the trends that are part of this opportunity, and you see that they're all long-term.** I've talked about the Baby Boomers; I've talked about business owners. And you can check out the samples we've provided in Section 3 of our free book and find that this really does have the potential to make hundreds of thousands of dollars a year — potentially even more. Now, that's not a promise or guarantee, but the potential is there, and the mathematical examples help to illustrate that it's solid.

Reason <u>NUMBER</u> <u>TEN</u> that CLUB-20 has the potential to make you rich: **you can make money with total privacy.**

Nobody has to know what you're doing. That's often not the case in business. Let's just look at a regular local business, for example. If you've got a store on Main Street, everybody will know your business — and everybody *should* know your business, because everybody in town might be a potential prospect. **But a lot of people want privacy.** They don't want their nosy neighbors to know what they're doing. This opportunity provides that kind of privacy. Maybe you don't want your family to know what you're doing, especially if you've been dragging your family and friends into other deals, so that now all of a sudden when they see you coming, they just pretend like they *don't* see you.

With CLUB-20, nobody has to know what you're doing to make money. **There's no personal selling. There's no contact with other people.** There's no talking to other people. You can, if you want to, of course. If part of your plan involves doing things that give you personal contact with people, that's your choice. But there's no need to. And in this day and age, privacy might be a good security thing, too. In this day and age, you might not *want* everybody to know what you're doing.

I live in a little town, and my house faces the main road

going in and out of town. I've got these windows that look out over the road. So in the winter time, especially, I go drink my coffee in the morning, and I look out the window and watch people going to work. I'm about an hour away from Wichita, and a lot of my neighbors work in Wichita, so they have an hour's drive every morning. Even at 5:30 in the morning, I'm watching all these cars drive by my house on their way to Wichita, because that's what they have to do — day, after day, after day. Once the sun comes up, I can really see them well, and I see the same cars going by every day. If that's the way people want to live, then more power to them. But I don't want to live like that. **I like being able to do everything from home. I go to the office very little.** And many other people are like me; they want something home-based, something private and personal. That's what we provide — a chance to work out of your house, to let us make money for you without facing rush-hour traffic. **You have total privacy and total security.** And when you do start rolling in the dough, just drive by and wink at your neighbors. Let them talk about you. They're going to talk and gossip about you anyway, so just give them a wink and a smile.

It all boils down to lifestyle. Beyond the security and privacy issues, a good, solid, home-based business can give you the lifestyle you want to live, where you're not locked into that 9-to-5 grind. Some people call it the "rat race." **CLUB-20 can give you the lifestyle you want — especially when you're looking for one where you don't have to deal with people.** It insulates you from having to go out and expose yourself to a lot of different elements that can come back and bite you. Because well, let's face it, in this economy there's a lot of crime going on. And you know the old saying: "Loose lips sink ships." Chris Hollinger was recently telling me that his neighbors went to church, and when they came back their big screen TV was gone. Their surround sound system was gone. All the computers in their house were gone, and so were a bunch of tools out of their garage. This all happened while they were at church — and Chris lives in a nice neighborhood. Obviously, somebody cased them and knew what they had. A lot of people think things like that don't happen in Kansas, but this isn't Mayberry.

With CLUB-20 you can make money in total privacy, and people don't have to know what it is you do, because you're not saying, "Hey, I've got this new opportunity. Come take a look at it." That's a good thing. **Our opportunity helps fulfill part of the market segment: those people that are really looking for a passive way to make money, where they don't have to be super-involved and broadcast the fact that they're doing it.** Now, sometimes people think, "Why would you hide what you're doing? Are you doing something shady you don't want people to know about?" They think that just because you want to be private, that means that you must be hiding something — and it's not that at all. It's just that today, especially, there's security in not having to have everybody know what you're up to. If people know you're successful, you're probably at more risk of theft.

And yet, you can choose to live a very modest lifestyle and still be making huge amounts of money. You don't have to move to a nicer neighborhood. You don't have to drive brand new cars. You can do whatever you want. A book titled *The Millionaire Next Door* by Thomas Stanley and William Danko exposes the myth that all successful people live extravagant lifestyles. **In fact, many of America's richest people look a lot like you and me.** They're average-looking. They dress in blue jeans. They don't drive brand new cars all the time. They're not driving fancy cars, either; they're driving Chevys and Ford pickup trucks. They don't live in million-dollar mansions; they live in modest homes. They choose to do things with their money like invest it, and they can buy anything they want, but they'd rather be normal.

Being private about your business affairs doesn't

223

necessarily mean you're trying to hide something. **In this day and age, it's good to be private.** With a lot of businesses, you're dealing with a situation where you've got to put signs on your van to help advertise yourself. Everybody knows what you do, because you rely on face-to-face publicity, word of mouth, people knowing who you are, and you're always out there in front of the public. Well, as a Direct-Response-style business, CLUB-20 allows you privacy. You can make money without anybody knowing what you're doing. You don't have to drag your friends and family into it; you can just live a low-key lifestyle, and enjoy the fruits of your success without having to have it be a big advertisement.

This is especially good for modest people who don't like to advertise their success — and yes, there are a lot of people like that. This business is not something where everybody has to even know how successful you are. You could literally be making millions of dollars from a spare bedroom in your home. You don't have to have a fancy office that everybody knows you work out of. You don't have to go out there and be a public figure, like you do with a lot of businesses. You don't have to deal with people wondering what you're doing, or people bothering you and asking for money, as sometimes happens when you're an obvious success.

Chapter Eight:

The Last Five Reasons

The <u>ELEVENTH</u> <u>REASON</u> CLUB-20 International has the power to make you rich is this: **the same people who have made us millions of dollars can now do everything for you.**

CLUB-20 uses the very same suppliers we've teamed with for years, people and companies that have made us huge sums of money. Now, let's go back chronologically to the very first few. In the beginning, back in September of 1988, my wife and I got off to a pretty good start. In the winter of 1988/1989, we got a letter from Russ von Hoelscher, who was a marketing consultant in our market. We already knew about him; I owned a copy of one of his books, *Selling Information By Mail*. By then we were making about $500 a day, on average, and Russ sent us a letter that said, "I like what you're doing. I think I can help you. Give me a call." He included his phone number and a brochure, so I called him up. Within 9 months our income shot from $500 a day—$16,000 a month, on average — to about $14,000 a day in sales. That's about $100,000 a week. We went on to bring in millions of dollars within just a few short years.

People always want to know: what's the one thing Russ did that helped us make more money than anything else? The truth is, he did a lot of things for us. He gave us his valuable contacts and shared information that had taken him over 20 years to learn. **But if there's one secret that did more for us than any other, it's that he got us involved in Direct-Mail.** Up until that time we were running small space ads in magazines. Then, with Russ's help, we started running full-page ads. And yet, it wasn't until we started doing Direct-Mail that our income just shot to the moon — and we've never looked back!

We do a tremendous amount of Direct-Mail Marketing to our customers. Once we generate leads, we mail relentlessly — millions and millions of pieces a year. **Just for new customer acquisition, we mail on the average of 25,000-50,000 pieces a week.** We used to slow down in the summertime and around Christmas, because everyone else did too; we assumed everyone was more interested in other things, especially during the holiday season. Now we just keep plowing right on through. Five or six years ago we decided to test during the Christmas holiday, and sure enough, our numbers were good. They held up, and one of the reasons I think they did is because everybody else was stopping, so we were the only ones showing up in people's mailboxes. From that point forward, 52 times a year, week after week, we're out there in their mailboxes.

Though we're doing millions of pieces of Direct-Mail, we're not mailing them ourselves. **We have a mailing house that takes care of all of that for us.** As I mentioned in Part I, we use a company called CCI, and we've been with them since 1991. When Russ first got us into Direct-Mail, we started out with a company out of Hutchinson, Kansas, that we discovered was cheating us. They were charging us for mailings that they weren't fulfilling, so we were paying for services they weren't performing. We found out about them real quick. So we called CCI, and ever since then, they've been our primary mailing house. I don't know how many tens of millions of pieces of mail they've mailed for us, but they take care of everything. They do it all for us — and they're partners in our business. They're not just a supplier that performs a service for us. Pam Fleming is our representative from CCI, and she shows up at our weekly meeting, week after week. She's like a staff member we don't have to pay. She makes suggestions, we implement them and make money, and it's really a win/win situation.

We've been working with the same printing company since 1994, City Print out of Wichita, Kansas. Our printer is Steve Harshbarger. He's another guy that's just like a partner of ours. He's more than a supplier; **he's somebody who looks out for our interests.** He really wants to help us. He's dedicated. He's committed. He's honest. He comes up with ways that we can save and make more money — and the better our company does, the better he does.

And then, last but not least, my staff helps us make money on a daily basis. **I've got a great staff.** I think they're the best; now, I might be biased, but I'm not all *that* biased. They're really good people. In large part, the secret to my success is based on two things: **1)** my willingness to do whatever it takes, and **2)** the fact that I've surrounded myself with the best people. If I had to list just two things that have been more responsible than anything else for us making millions of dollars, it's those two things. We're known by the people we surround ourselves with, and I've surrounded myself with some extremely high-caliber folks who are smarter and more talented than I am, and I'm striving to be a better person as a result.

All those people I've mentioned — **the suppliers, our staff members — will also be working on your behalf when you become part of our team.** Our infrastructure is like a pipeline that produces dollars. They're very good at what they do, and they can do it all for you. So if you don't want to sit there putting labels on mailers, have CCI do it. In one fell swoop, they can put an envelope through their machine, put sizzling copy on it, address it, and put postage on it. It goes out as a really good-looking mailing. The printers and list brokers are also very important, and you'll be using the same ones we do.

That infrastructure is key, and with CLUB-20, it's

already a pipeline that's up and running. They're good people, and they know what they're doing. And the neat thing is, you plug right into them automatically. Normally, when you think about infrastructure, you think of bad things like overhead and high costs and all that. Infrastructure costs money. Think about the problems at General Motors, for instance. Ford has been able to avoid government intervention, but to some degree, they suffer from the same thing. They call it "legacy costs, overhead, infrastructure." Most businesses look at it as a bad thing. We're one of the few businesses in the opportunity market that can support it, **because the infrastructure we maintain helps us help our clients make money.** It benefits everybody.

Another problem you see with a lot of companies is that they jump around from one vendor and supplier to another; the vendors they use today are not the vendors they're using tomorrow. They're always looking for the cheapest thing out there. **But with suppliers, if you go cheap, you get what you pay for.** We don't use the cheapest suppliers. There are suppliers who would charge us less, and we've had some of them approach us for business. **But we use what we feel is the best, and the companies we use know Direct-Mail, because they specialize in it.** They work with our list brokers to get us the best mailing lists. They're constantly involved in our day-to-day operations. They've been doing that for us for many years — before we ever really started thinking about putting together systems that would help our clients benefit from that. We don't give you guys access to cut-rate suppliers so we can continue our relationship with our good suppliers. **You get to use the same suppliers we're using.**

Another part of our infrastructure is our in-house support system. A lot of companies out-source a lot of stuff, and sometimes that can be okay. It certainly can save money sometimes. But we have an internal staff that does things for us that benefits *you*, as well. We have a shipping department that's able to expand to meet our needs — and yours. We have crews who come in occasionally when we've got big mailings, so that room is just full of assembly line tables where they're running through and stuffing envelopes and getting packages ready to mail. Whenever one of your prospects for CLUB-20 requests the free book, that request goes straight to our shipping department, and they ship that package ASAP — usually within 24 hours. **We get those packages out fast, because everything is controlled at the epicenter of all the activity of our business: our headquarters.** We also have a full administrative staff. When people request the book and those leads come in off the website, that all gets processed *immediately* so that we can get those packages shipped out.

Then, once your prospect comes into the system and they're getting follow-ups, they get calls from our sales reps. **Remember, we talked about how they're working for you.** Those client service representatives are on the phone all day long, up to six days a week, especially in the evenings. They're also there early in the morning, all to call and work with your clients and try to get them to purchase. We pay those salespeople really well to do a good job, and we train them extremely well. We have Drew Hanson to manage them and make sure they're doing an effective job, to make sure they're working honorably and that they're telling the truth at all times. There have been stories of sales departments that were just trying to make a sale. Well, we don't want someone *just* trying to make a sale. We want them to do it honorably, to work with the clients on the up-and-up. Drew manages all that, to make sure that's happening.

We've also got a great management team. I've got six people on my management team besides myself: Chris Lakey, Drew Hanson, Jeff McMannis, my stepson Chris, Randy Hamilton (our numbers guy who's been with us almost 20 years), and Felicia Crosby, my shipping manager. I'm proud of these people. They're very, very good people! **And here's the point: nobody ever gets rich by themselves.** I know that that may sound like common sense, yet I see so many people who think they can get rich alone. They truly have the desire to make millions of dollars — and yet they're stubborn, independent, and difficult to work with, and they so badly want to do everything themselves that everything I know about making millions of dollars isn't going to work for them! Some of them are extremely bright, too. In fact, they're *too* damn smart. Because they're too smart, they want to do it all, just because they can. Me, I don't know how to do very much of anything. I'm only good at a couple of things, and that's it. So I naturally need other people filling in all the gaps. I'm proud of our team.

We have friends of who change suppliers like you and I change our underwear. Any time they can get a cheaper price, they switch. They're never loyal to any of their suppliers — and their suppliers aren't loyal to them, either. They're always looking for the best deal for the best price, so they have multiple vendors that they give their stuff to — and they have no real relationship with any of them. A relationship is more than just ordering a service. It's thick and thin, back and forth, give and take. **I feel we've done a very good job of forming solid relationships with the people we do business with, and that includes a good stable staff, people that have been with us year after year.** Some companies have a problem with turnover; we have the exact opposite problem.

And then there's our list broker. The most important ingredient for all Direct-Mail success has nothing to do with the mail at all; **the most important ingredient is the mailing list you use.** We've been using the same mailing list broker since Russ first introduced us to him in early 1990. His name is Stuart Cogan, with MegaMedia in Anaheim, California. I've never met

Stuart, but he's been doing a wonderful job for all this time.

Reason <u>NUMBER</u> <u>TWELVE</u> that CLUB-20 has the power to make you rich: **you have an almost unfair advantage over all the people who are already getting rich in similar opportunities.**

I've already talked about the fact that there are already plenty of companies using this new type of comp plan, which pays the largest commissions to the smallest number of distributors. I've already covered the three big advantages that you have over them, but I'll mention them quickly again, because they're worth re-emphasizing.

NUMBER 1: We look at sales as a process, not an event. Those companies are trying to sell too much, too fast. They're trying to take a prospect from cold to hot too quickly. As a result, the prospects feel high-pressured, and high-pressured prospects aren't likely to buy. That's the biggest mistake these companies make: they're trying to travel from A to Z without hitting all those letters in between, and they're losing a lot of money in the process. That's wasteful marketing, and it's stupid. It's done by people who don't know what they're doing. That's like going to a first year medical student and asking them to perform major surgery on you. You'd never do it. It would be a dumb move. These people just don't know what the hell they're doing, that's all.

NUMBER 2: They're involved in personal selling, which is the hardest way to make money. I've done personal selling — that's how I got started. I've mentioned how I originally worked in the factories and construction and oil fields. What initially got me out of the factories was personal selling. I didn't start my first business till 1985, but about two years before that I got my first sales job. I worked in sales departments, and I went through many sales jobs. **I learned that**

personal selling is a hard way to make money. Most people don't want to do it, first of all, so it's not very duplicable. Most people *can't* do it. And even for the people who can, there are smarter ways to make money. We know those ways.

Personal selling is a young man's game. When my colleague Chris Hollinger was in college, he would go out and sell and install gutter guard on people's houses. When he walked up to someone's door with the flyer he'd typed up and printed on the university computer, he would hope a woman answered. If a woman did answer, he knew he had his ideal prospect, because most guys were like, "Hell no. I'm going to clean up my own gutters, and I'll take care of that." Now, Chris bought that gutter guard for 9.9 cents a running foot, and he installed it for somewhere upwards of $1.50 to $2 a running foot, so he was making good money for a 20-year-old college student. But he says he wouldn't want to do that type of personal selling nowadays.

Direct-Response takes that whole personal equation out of it. You're not sitting there on the phone asking people, "Okay, are you ready to spend some money?" Most people don't like personal selling like that. They don't have the tenacity it takes to stay on the phones to build a business that way. **Direct-Response allows you to develop a prospect, close that prospect, and not have to even know or ever talk to them.** It's a very beautiful thing. And when you have a whole marketing system that's based on Direct-Response, you've got something powerful, something that has a dramatic advantage over the vast majority of Network Marketing opportunities. You don't have to bug friends, or families, or complete strangers with what I call an "elevator speech." **There are better ways of doing it, and Direct-Response is that answer.**

Now, I'll be the first person to admit that personal selling can work. Chris Hollinger recently told me about a fellow who

232

sold him insurance years ago. In the months leading up to his oldest daughter's birth, Chris and his wife took some classes on childcare and Lamaze. That was 13 years ago. One of the guys in that class with his pregnant wife was an insurance salesman, and he was handing out cards. At that time, life insurance was at the top of Chris' mind. He had a young family and needed to take care of them. So Chris ended up buying life insurance from him, and he still has the policy today, though the salesman is now out of the business. But there he was, making connections with people that he met. That's the way a lot of Network Marketing opportunities work.

The THIRD mistake those people are making is that they have no marketing system, so it's all hit and miss, feast or famine, up and down. It's a roller coaster ride. There's no stable income, because there's no real marketing system driving it all. Traditional MLM has what they call the three-foot rule. That means every time you come within three feet of somebody, you're supposed to be slamming them on your business opportunity. You're supposed to be bugging everybody. They do all kinds of things to supposedly help you do that, like giving you buttons you're supposed to wear that say "Lose Weight Now... Ask Me How," or some dumb thing like that. You're supposed to be pitching everybody you come into contact with about your product or service. **That's no way to live.**

We have advantages over local businesses, too. In many cases, local businesses aren't a good idea for several reasons. **But the first reason is that you're limited by your local market.** So if you really want to get rich, you've got to have a wider appeal. I've mentioned this couple I know in Hesston, Kansas, a few times already. They've got a great coffee shop, and if you ever happen to go to Hillsboro, you should go there. This lady serves great coffee and offers great service. She's just a beautiful person, and she's really doing a good job. And yet, she's barely making it financially — and frankly, I'm shocked that she's still in business, because Hillsboro is just a tiny market area. There are only so many people there, so her market is limited.

In many ways, we're like a franchise. Think about what a franchise does: they make their money by helping their franchisees make money. They collect a percentage of every dollar, and they provide all kinds of support services. A good franchise will do everything it can to help you make money, because you're one of their family, so to speak, and because they've got a strong vested interest. The more they can do to see to it that you make a lot of money, the more money they make.

And yet franchises have three strikes against them. First, they're still limited by your market area. That's never good. Second, the fees you have to pay to acquire a good franchise can be in the six figures, easily. So you've got to shell out tens or even hundreds of thousands of dollars before you take in your first dollar of profit. That puts you at a significant disadvantage. Third, any self-respecting entrepreneur would never be caught dead with a franchise, because they impose all kinds of rules on you. One of the reasons we're in business is so we can have some freedom!

CLUB-20 is a distributorship. You're free to experiment with your own ideas. If you find something that's really working well for you, well... don't tell me about it, because I'm an open book, and I'll tell everybody! Do we want to know that you're adhering to certain guidelines and not doing anything that might be questionable in the eyes of the regulatory agencies that monitor us? Yes. But you're not going to do anything that questionable anyway, right? **We want you to have freedom, even while we help you prosper by doing as much as we can.**

There are some new companies out there that are coming up with new ways to do business, and they're trying to be cutting edge. But here's what they do: They give you a website and tell you, "Hey, you want to be on the Internet!" You don't have to talk to your warm market anymore, and you don't have to follow franchise rules, but all you have is a website, which is supposed to do *everything* for you. And sometimes it does; some of these companies have great products and great websites. **But there's no Direct-Response system; there's no follow-up.** You bring people to the website, and maybe they sign up and maybe they don't, but that's it. Maybe they watch a video. You don't really have any way to capture their contact information and send them any follow-up mail. They don't even do Direct-Mail... they discourage you from doing it, in fact. They might tell you it's expensive, and you should avoid that. That's what the Internet is for, right?

We've actually tested some Internet advertising and found that Direct-Mail is better for our business model — and we've done very well at it. **That's why we feel the better approach is a two-step marketing system where, either through a website or through Direct-Mail, you capture a lead** — that is, you get someone to request more information from you (like our free *$60,000 in 90 Days* book), and from there you follow up with them over and over and encourage them to buy from you. **That kind of system gives you an almost unfair advantage over all the companies** that have systems that either rely on your warm market or give you a website that's supposed to do everything in the selling process for you.

The <u>THIRTEENTH</u> <u>REASON</u> that CLUB-20 International has the ability to make you rich is: because **all of the money comes to you very, very quickly.** You'll never have to worry if the company behind the opportunity is paying you every single penny of your money.

I'm a distributor right now for two traditional MLM companies that I really believe in, and I love these companies.

I'm committed and dedicated, and yet I know that, in the past, there have been plenty of committed, dedicated distributors who have built huge downlines like the one we're planning to build, and then they've gotten the rug pulled out from under them. In fact, I've been thrown out of a couple of MLM companies already. What happens is, you build a huge downline. A large amount of money is supposed to come due to you every month, now that you've got hundreds or thousands of distributors that you've put into the opportunity. Every month, you're supposed to be getting a big check. **But then they find reasons to throw you out, or you decide you want to get out for other reasons.** For example, there was an opportunity that I was involved in that was based out of Los Angeles, California. We brought in over a thousand distributors and were supposed to be collecting money every month. And yet, at the end of the day, we just walked away from it. We're the ones who made the decision to walk away from that deal. We left a lot of business on the table, because we didn't want to do business with those people anymore. We took a lot of our distributors with us, too.

A lot of companies pay monthly, and that may be okay; you can work within that framework, if that's the way they do it. But what ends up happening is, you work an entire month to earn commissions, and then the company has to do their accounting and figure out how many sales you made. **They take three or four weeks to figure that out, so it's maybe four, or five, or six weeks before the check actually arrives in the mail.** They're always paying you a month to a month and a half behind. **You're always waiting to get paid.** And if something happens and the relationship goes sour, they're sitting on a bunch of your money.

That doesn't happen with CLUB-20. **The bottom line is, you get paid quickly.** And the metaphor that I like to think about is this: In front of my house is this pond. And although I like it, it's all muddy. One of the reasons it's brown and muddy is because there's no flow coming through. Now, on his property, Chris Lakey has a pond that's spring-fed, so he's got a stream that comes through it, and a stream that goes out. His pond isn't muddy like my pond is. My pond is all stagnated, and you can't even see what's underneath there. You don't even want to swim in it, because you can't see what's there. Chris's pond is transparent, and the water comes in and goes out quickly — like the money does in CLUB-20. We pay quickly. **We send out checks four days a week, Monday through Thursday.** As soon as a sale clears, your check goes out the very next payday. It's like a clear-running stream. We just give you all the money right up front.

Getting money in people's pockets actually makes the company more money. That seems like it would be a no-brainer, but I've been involved with companies in the past where it seems like you're just pulling teeth to get your check from them. **This is one thing that truly differentiates CLUB-20 International from so many opportunities.**

We're not rule-bound, either. A lot of opportunities will kick you out if you're not following their rules exactly. When you sign up, you get this thick rule book that's about 50 pages long. It's full of all the rules, regulations, and guidelines you're supposed to follow. They only want you doing things exactly the way they say you should do things. They hope you succeed; they want you to do well, of course. But they want you to do well by their book, and they want you to follow their rules. And they want you to only advertise the exact way they *say* you can advertise. We've been kicked out of companies, because we didn't follow their rules on how they wanted you to advertise. Well, we feel it's our business, and we're promoting their product; we should be able to advertise it however we want to. But they try to pin you down with this narrow scope, and if you don't follow their rules, they don't like it. That's where a lot of the rub comes in with distributors and various MLM companies. When you try to do things your way, they slap you down. Well, hey! A lot of entrepreneurs are independent. That's part of being an entrepreneur, and they don't like that. **Well, we know that entrepreneurs want to have the freedom to work within their own style and do things the way they like to do things, so we let them.** Now, we have a few rules and regulations that you have to follow as a distributor, but those are basic: **we want you to keep things on the up-and-up. We want you to follow certain very loosely-structured guidelines.** But otherwise, we give you complete freedom to be an entrepreneur.

That's one of the reasons we give you the ability to generate leads however you want to. **We don't encourage you to do it just one way.** We have our automated system that lets you give away a free book, but that's not the only way you can do it. **We also have a website that includes videos, and it just sells the product. You're welcome to use that.** You can give away the free book by mailing postcards, buying classified ads, talking to people — doing whatever you want. Or, we can give you some eBook websites that you can give away. You can use those to generate leads and get people to request the book. You could come up with a completely unique system based on your own ideas for how you think things should run. **We'd like you to run it by us, because maybe we have some suggestions for you, but it doesn't matter to us if you want to use your own system.** Now, of course, **we've perfected what we feel is a pretty powerful automated system that we encourage you to use.** But we don't require you to do so. That's what makes us different.

Some opportunities will claim that they'll let you market the way you want — and then back off on that claim when you start making money. Here's a good example from Chris Hollinger. When he gets involved with an opportunity, he's always careful to contact their director of marketing and advertising. He'll say something like, "Look, this is a full-page ad that I want to run. Is it okay? Run this by Compliance and make sure." He'll get a go-ahead, it'll run, and he'll start generating leads on it — and then maybe one of their big-wig distributors from another part of the country will see Chris' ad and say, "Well, he can't do that!" And so the company will come back to Chris and say, "Well, no, you can't run it," after they already gave him the go-ahead, and he's already run it for a month. Those things happen. There's a human element that gets involved in here; people are people, and somebody might gripe about it. **FYI, a good way around that is to run blind ads, where you don't mention that particular company at all.** These ads are designed to generate a lead so you can follow it up with a mailing packet that *does* have approved ad materials in it.

But the point is, you can get in sticky situations where you *think* you're doing everything fine, and the next thing you know they didn't like something — and there's some fine print somewhere they can nail you on. If you're like me, you like the whole idea of freedom, of being the master of your own destiny, of being allowed to choose some of the marketing and advertising that you want to use. **That's why CLUB-20 rises head and shoulders above the competition.**

Reason <u>NUMBER</u> <u>FOURTEEN</u> that CLUB-20 has the power to make you rich: **The market is still untapped; it's still the ground floor.**

Very often, the problem with new companies is the fact that they're new. That may not sound very profound, but if you think about it, the fact that they're new means that they're unproven, they're untested, and they don't have the infrastructure in place yet. There are too many unknowns, too many variables. **Well, the neat thing about CLUB-20 is that we're a brand new opportunity, and yet we're backed by a company that's over 20 years old. We have a proven track record of success,**

utilizing the very best of the best of the marketing systems that we've developed and perfected over those two decades. While we *are* a new company, we're built on a foundation that goes back to 1988.

And again, the market is largely untapped. Certainly, there have been people selling seminars for many years; that's not anything new. **The Wealth Explosion Seminars we're going to be having, though, build on something new and different that hasn't been available before.** We've never done a seminar like we'll be doing. They will be brand new, bringing in new people, and doing things in a different way. All this will certainly be new to a lot of the people that will be entering this market. I've already talked at length about the two main marketplaces we're serving: **Baby Boomers and all the small business owners** who are struggling, especially in this economy. There are more and more people every day looking to start a business — either to counter the recession, or to supplement their income, or just to keep themselves busy as they near retirement and start having more time freed up in their schedule. All of those people will be looking for a new opportunity like CLUB-20.

Americans love new. Our whole country was founded on the New World. It's always been a part of our history, part of our culture, even as our culture has changed over the years. That's why you see so many marketers put "All New!" or something similar on their products. The best unique example of this is laundry detergent. Laundry detergent really hasn't changed for a long, long time, but Tide and Cheer are always coming out with an "All New" version: the scented, the unscented, the re-scented, the fresh scented, the stain fighter, whatever. It's *all new*. They're always *all new!* But the basic product itself is the same as it's always been. **So we've got our own "All New!" to offer with CLUB-20. But at the same time, it's got the history and culture of an established winner behind it — a 20-year track**

record of success. It's what makes us unique.

We've been around since 1988, true enough, **but it's only been since 2006 that we've had our sales department put together in a solid way — and it's revolutionized our entire company.** It's amazing to us how we were able to somehow manage and make really good money for all those years without having a good, solid sales department. I'll make a bold prediction that we're part of a trend here. I predict that in the future, every company that does Direct-Response Marketing is going to definitely have to have a sales department to pick up all of the business that they're losing without one.

Now, let's talk about some of the complexities of building a sales department. One of the most complex things is simply finding the right people. You can find people who want to sell; you can find people who want to make a lot of money. **But the hard thing is finding somebody who wants to do it *your* way and who wants to be part of *your* team.** Not only do they have to work well for you and work well for us, but they have to work well together. Everybody has to get along.

When they're working for you, when they're calling your clients and working on your behalf, **they have to care — and they have to want for you to succeed. And then they have to, in turn, want to help your customer succeed.** It's an ever-flowing cycle, and that takes a special person who's not just going to go in there and go through the motions. We don't need people who'll just pick up the phone and say, "Hey, did you get the manual? Great. Do you want to buy it? Okay, have a good day." There are people that will do that. What's going to make you the most money is having that person on the phone for you who's going to find out what your customer's objection is, who's going to find out what's it going to take to get a deal put together for *you* so that you can have a person on your team. And that, by far, is the hardest thing of building a team like this:

241

finding somebody that has that commitment and that passion — not only for themselves, but for you.

We have weekly meetings with the sales staff to make sure that that dynamic is there, and I know that Drew makes an effort to make sure that everybody stays on the same page and are all working together. Anytime you have a bunch of people working together, there's the potential for rubbing each other the wrong way. Emotions and interoffice politics can get in the way of doing the job. We have a meeting every week to talk about what's going well, what's not going well, what our challenges and struggles are, and how we can help the sales staff as they talk to clients. While they work to build relationships with our clients, we help them make sure that they're doing that as effectively as possible.

About15 years ago, my wife went through a stage where she raised quarter horses. They're beautiful animals! I like driving by and watching them. But I used to have to take care of them. My job was to feed them and clean out their stalls... and I don't miss that! But they're the most magnificent creatures, just beautiful. And yet, the one thing about horses is that they're extremely temperamental. It doesn't take much to set them off at all. I mean, you clap too loud, and all of a sudden they attack you or they'll run right over you. Well, as I see it, good salespeople are like these very temperamental, beautiful quarter horses. **Being a telephone sales person is probably the hardest work that I personally know of.** Day after day, you're getting on the telephone and dealing with people who are often difficult. At best you're getting a lot of no's from people; often people are saying, "Don't you call me back *ever again!*" And it gets worse; use your imagination, if you will.

Starting out, you just about panic. I'll never forget the first day that I started doing telephone sales. You start talking to a customer, and it's like the first time you've ever talked to anybody in your life. It's hard work, especially since it goes on day after day. Anybody can do it for a short period of time; I'm convinced of that. Some people could probably do it for a week or two, and some people might even be able to do it for a couple months. But to do it day after day requires constant training, supervision, and encouragement. **You've got to put systems in place to keep people motivated. If you get it right, and find that right balance of temperament, you can keep going for years.** We have one guy who probably has 15 years of experience, another who's pushing 20. Once you're trained and you've spent enough time on the phone, you tend to understand how it all works and it becomes second nature — to the point where you can call somebody and just start having a conversation where you're getting to know them. It's a process, and sure, it can be tedious. Sometimes our very first call is just something like, "Hey, I'm Drew. How's it going? Where are you from, and what do you like to do? I'm here for ya…" and there's not even an attempt to say anything about the system or anything like that. A lot of times that's what it takes.

So when we're working behind the scenes with one of your clients, it can be weeks before a sale is made. **Progress is being made the entire time, but it can take a long time to build a relationship,** to build trust, to get an idea of their personality, to learn what they like to do, and build a bond before you even start to try to say, "Okay, let's get this thing going." That relationship takes time, and it can be very frustrating. Some days are good; some days it's like every call you make, there's some magic. And then there are other days, sometimes even weeks, when nothing you can do seems to work.

But the motivation and inspiration in our group often comes down to numbers. **We know we have a good product, and we know that a certain percentage of people will buy.** The very next person you talk to could be the one. You can't let yourself be down; it takes tremendous discipline to not make that next call just horrible, just by being down. People can hear that through the phone. So you've got to maintain that mentality, of knowing that the next one could be the one. That's really hard to do, especially when you're new.

But as far as keeping the salespeople motivated, we do lots of other things. We'll have a little contest or something to get them going, get them excited. For instance, we might say, "Hey, this week we'll pay for a massage from Ray Prieba if you meet this goal," so that gets them going and gets them on the phone. **We constantly have to come up with either a contest, or just sit down and take a breather and talk about the problems the rep is having.** Sometimes we'll even sit down and make some calls together, so they can hear a different person make a call to the same client, and sometimes that makes a difference. We have our own little toolbox of things that we pull out when a rep is disgruntled or having a slow day. We have lots of things we use for that.

A good salesman can adapt to anything. My colleague Chris Hollinger recently told me about a person he worked with in college who was a real chameleon. He was a psychology major and could change his stripes depending on who he was talking to. Chris told me about one time when he saw him talking to lawyers early in the day; he had his three-piece suit on, talking to them on their level. Later, they drove to a small town to meet with a couple who owned a convenience store, and those folks were sitting there smoking cigarettes. The next thing Chris knew, the other guy was smoking cigarettes and drinking their beer! There was a reason why he was such a good personal salesman: **he could adapt to any situation.** As soon as he drove into that town and got out of his car, he took his jacket off and undid his tie before he walked in, because he knew the type of people he was going to be meeting with. He was able to instantly connect with a person.

But not every salesperson is going to be a chameleon from the word go. Most start out being nervous. The first call is probably not going to go well, unless they've been at it for a while and had other experience, so you've got to have those mechanisms in place to get them over that hump. That's one thing we offer in spades with CLUB-20. Our department is quite amazing; I've seen it in action many times, and they do a great job.

Now, I do want to say that all of those years when we didn't have a sales department, that didn't mean that we weren't bringing salespeople in, because we were. We brought a bunch of salespeople in to *try* to do what Drew has done so successfully. The thing that I know now that I didn't know then, hindsight being 20/20, is that I happen to the world's worst manager. **I don't have the qualities of a good manager —** particularly the qualities of maturity, common sense, and stability. So we would hire salespeople, and they would work out for a little while, but then they would go through a learning curve and would have some problems. Then they would quit — and I didn't know how to control that. Drew Hanson constantly works with every salesperson he brings on board. Inevitably, they do go through a time when it looks like they could quit. Drew will let them struggle for a little while, just so that they can see everything that they're doing wrong. **And then, basically, he tries to teach through that and show that things are always going to be uncomfortable.** You never get to a point where it's completely easy.

First, we teach the rep about all the products. **Product knowledge is the first thing we focus on, because they have to be fully comfortable with that to be any good at selling.** If you don't know all the answers, and if you don't know the products forwards and backwards, then you're going to do more harm than good. Once they know the products, we'll put them on the phone for a while, making calls without much direction. They may do that for half a day. This allows us to cater to the rep's presentation, based on how they handle themselves.

I'm sure everybody has talked to a telemarketer who just sits there and reads right down a script. They all sound exactly the same; they have the same voice inflection, the same tone. We don't work that way. By finding out what the rep is having a hard time with, we can then build to their personality. Not a single one of our reps is exactly alike, and so not one of them can give the very same presentation. The reason they go through an initial struggle is so we can customize the way they work with your customers, so that they can do their best job possible. That makes them more natural, as if they're not scripted at all. **They can basically just go out there and be the best salesperson that *they* can be, and we're not forcing them to say everything line-by-line.** That makes your customers feel more comfortable.

Drew helped me realize the importance of having a good sales manager. **Being a sales manager has a whole different set of requirements than being a general manager, the first is that you have to be a salesman yourself.** You can't hire a regular manager to manage your sales department; you have to have somebody who has a good sales background. Well, I had that. But they also have to be a good manager in the first place, which I'm not. That's the reason why, for years, we had salespeople come and go. Every few years we'd hire a couple new ones, they'd stay a while, and then they would leave. It was my fault. We didn't have the right management in place.

We encourage the salespeople and let them know how much we appreciate them. We're always looking for ways to incentivize them and get them excited. We have contests constantly. In fact, as I write this we've got a huge contest running. The salesperson who sells the most tickets for our first Wealth Explosion Seminar on August 7-9 gets a week's paid vacation anywhere they want to go. Think about that! Now, there may be some restrictions; but they can go anywhere within the United States, or down to a resort in Mexico. We currently have three salespeople who are neck-and-neck. They're getting excited, and you can just feel the vibrations in there. I mean, they're pumped up! They're jazzed! And they're working about 500 million times harder than they normally work, because they all want to make more money. **They get a commission, of course, every time they make a sale.** Every time they make $1,000 for you, they get $225-250 dollars. So they're incentivized to work as hard as they can to make money for you.

How we were able to make it all those years without a good team of salespeople is beyond me. **Being totally dependent on Direct-Mail for all those years, we were losing a lot of money that could, and should, have been ours.** I think the days are gone when somebody can run a Direct-Response Marketing company of any size and not have a good solid sales department. Companies doing that are just leaving all kinds of revenue right on the table that could, and should, be theirs. **They're just not following up.** It takes more and more to sell people these days, what with competition being fiercer and with people being more skeptical.

If you start piecing together a lot of this stuff that I've been sharing with you, **you get a pretty good idea of why a lot of people who get involved in Network Marketing fail.** I've talked about so many elements that go into getting a prospect to raise their hand and say they want to know more information, and then the process or system that's involved in actually getting them to say "yes" once, and then to say "yes" again and again. **This is where a sales department becomes a must.** When I mentioned earlier that a lot of people try to go too fast too soon, it's absolutely true. You have to take it easy and massage the system on a daily basis to get the most out of it. Whereas, so many people who get in Network Marketing act like, "I've got to make money right now!" They don't understand that people don't jump from Point A to Point B just because you say so. And just because *you* have enthusiasm for something doesn't mean somebody else does. **So our system is designed to take them through the process of making up their minds gradually, and ultimately, get them to that answer we all like: "Yes!"**

I believe contacting people on the phone and actually speaking to them is a good idea, and it's becoming more and more common. **More marketers are starting to ask for phone numbers.** They don't always use them, but they're asking for them. **One thing I think is great about our system is that every customer who requests information from us is going to get a phone call.** And that's because we have an entire staff that does nothing else all day long. We honestly believe that more and more people are going to start doing this. In fact, Drew Hanson was recently interviewed for a magazine article, and he said, "More and more, you're going to see people trying to emulate our system. But they're going to really have a big surprise coming when they find out **a)** how much work it takes, and **b)** how much it costs to put something like this together." I think we've put together a phenomenal system, and we're proud now to be able to offer it to you. It's a way that you can rely on us to make the most money for *you*.

Okay, I've covered 14 of the 15 reasons why CLUB-20 International has the power to make you very, very rich. NUMBER FIFTEEN is last, but not least. It's the fact that **this is a unique wealth-making system that contains 27 key advantages that separates it from almost every other business opportunity**.

Our company has been researching business opportunities

professionally since September 1988. In fact, the real name of our company is "Mid-American Opportunity Research Enterprises, Inc." M.O.R.E. is just an acronym that we like to use, because we want to give our customers MORE, MORE, and even MORE! For 20+ years, we've been investigating and researching all kinds of different moneymaking opportunities and business opportunities.

Now, I've already gone over these points in Chapter 4 of Part I, so I won't repeat all that information again. However, I *am* going to reiterate what I think are the **top eight of those 27 advantages. The FIRST is this: Most opportunities use the same boring plans and programs that will never make you rich.**

We see the same stuff over and over again. It's boring. It's tired. It's been out there a long time. There's nothing new about it. People are doing the same things they've been doing for years. Well, in order to get people excited, you've got to have something new, something that captivates them, something that gets them excited, something that motivates them, something that inspires them. **For us, it's that concept of $60,000 in 90 days.** That's something that cuts through the clutter. It separates itself from all of the other dull messages, gives people something new, gets their attention and interest, and it gets them excited.

We built CLUB-20 from the ground up to be an exciting opportunity, so that it wouldn't have this problem of being the same as everything else. You see this stultifying sameness happening, sometimes, when one company does something unique and enjoys a little success. All of a sudden, everybody else is selling a product that looks similar, sounds similar, does the same thing, offers the same benefits — especially in the world of health products, like vitamins and juices. When one company tastes success, pretty soon up pop a bunch of other ones that are all very similar. Their bottles look a little different, and the name is different, but the structure of the company is the same. The product offers some of the same benefits, and it offers to cure some of the same ailments.

By the way, you've got to be careful with saying that you'll cure ailments. Here's a good example: Cheerios. The FDA, through FTC enforcement, has said now that Cheerios is a drug, because Cheerios claims to reduce your cholesterol. By making that claim, they're no longer just a food; it's not just Cheerios anymore, thanks to our government regulators. **You've got to be careful when you make such claims; those things are highly regulated.**

CLUB-20 offers a new product. Our Wealth Explosion Seminars are something that people can't get anywhere else. Even though other companies do seminars, have coaching programs, and teach marketing; none of them do it the way we do it, and none have our experience and our history to offer. There's nothing boring, plain, or tired about CLUB-20. However, as I've mentioned before, one problem with new things is that they're untested and unproven. Well, again, we've fixed that too! Here we have an opportunity that's brand new, and yet it's backed with the foundation of a 20-year-old company that's providing the same marketing systems and tools that we've used for many years now to generate millions of dollars. So that's unique.

The SECOND advantage we have over most business opportunities is that they force you to work long hours with little pay.

Most people are working way too hard for way too little money. They get into business because they have a dream of being their own bosses. That dream turns into a nightmare, because they're working long hours and they're not making enough money to pay their bills. They're taking enormous risks.

But we have an opportunity that's set up to pay people quickly, and it's a real partnership, since you're doing part of the work while we're doing the rest. **We make our money by helping you, period.** The faster we can put cash into your pocket, the faster we can put cash into our own. This system was built to have as little involvement on your part as possible.

The problem with most opportunities is that when you buy in, you buy little more than a job. They force you to wear lots of hats, too. **The benefit of CLUB-20 is that we have an automated system that can do everything for you.** We have a back-end marketing system that closes all the sales, works with your clients — all that. There's only one step for you to take, and we can even take care of that, too. You're getting paid on other things besides the number of hours you work — and that's the key to making a fortune. In fact, it gives you an opportunity to make a fortune part-time, which is almost unheard of in most business opportunities.

Number THREE: Most business opportunities force you to become a salesperson.

Often, people get started in a business because they enjoy the kinds of products and services the business provides. And yet, what they find is that they have to become a salesperson in order to make any substantial amounts of money. Now, I love salespeople. I value them. I appreciate what they do. My favorite people in the whole world are salespeople. And part of the reason for that is because I know how extremely difficult it is to do what they do, day in and day out.

Most businesspeople have no interest in becoming a salesperson whatsoever. And yet, they get started in business and find that it's really not about who has the better product or service; it's about who's the better salesperson. People think that, just because they can provide a higher level of product or service, people are going to naturally flock to them, and yet, in a competitive market it never happens that way. The squeaky wheel gets the grease. **The best marketer gets the money.** If we were all salespeople, we'd all be able to write our own paychecks, and we'd all be able to sell just about anything. But being a salesperson is a specialized skill that not just anybody can develop. If you can't, you're forced to figure everything out on your own, or you're forced to hire an ad agency or somebody else who can take care of that for you.

Well, you've already seen that this isn't a problem with CLUB-20, since **you've got a system in place where our salespersons do the work for you.** One of the things people who teach Direct-Mail will tell you is that each envelope you send out is like a salesperson that goes door-to-door, making the presentation, closing the sale, taking the order, and leaving. It leaves by way of the order form being mailed or faxed back to the company. **With Direct-Mail, you're able to let the mail be your salesperson,** and you can have thousands of salespeople going out all over the country, so you don't have to be a salesperson yourself. We've got a complete system that does all of the selling and, therefore, none of our distributors have to do any selling. So it's a real advantage.

The FOURTH reason CLUB-20 is better than all those other opportunities is that while most opportunities pay you small sums of money and no residual income, that's not true for CLUB-20.

Most businesspeople wake up on the first morning of every month with a real nightmare ahead of them, because they've got bills coming in — and they have to start fresh every single month, right back from zero again. How are they going to cover all of their bills? When it's all brand new and the enthusiasm and excitement levels are high, they might be able to sustain it. But after a while, it just runs them down. **I've seen so many small**

businesspeople have the dream turn into a nightmare. They're selling products and services for small amounts of money, with thin profit margins, in over-competitive markets, with no residual income. Some of the opportunities we've investigated pay just a dollar or two on every sale. The products themselves don't cost that much — it's a $30 bottle of pills or a $50 bottle of juice. There's just not that much commission to pay. You're forced to make thousands of sales and bring in thousands of distributors before you ever make any real money.

Well, it doesn't take many $1,000 commissions to add up to huge sums of money. On top of that, you're also getting paid $1,000 for every sale that's made for you by the people we place into your team. **So it's got leverage built into it; the system keeps it going steadily, and it has the potential to bring you money month after month.** It comes in without your direct effort, as long as you and your distributors are using the marketing system.

Number FIVE: Most opportunities cannot be handled from the comfort, privacy, and safety of your own home.

It's a dangerous world out there! It's best if you can have something that's private, something you can do out of your home, **where the amount of money you make isn't dependent on the number of hours you actually put in.** That's the kind of opportunity we have. It's just paradise. You can stay home, and your lifestyle doesn't necessarily have to revolve around your business. That's unlike the way most business people live. It's all just about business; there's no life left over.

Now, it's not that you really want to hide your business, or that you mind telling people what you do. It's just that most people do like to be private. Most people don't like to be bothered. Think about most local businesses — especially local

253

service businesses — where they drive around in a truck with their logo on the side, and everybody knows they're the local plumber or the local electrician. Those people live very public lives, because they have to. Everybody knows who they are and what they do.

With CLUB-20, no one has to know what you're doing. **You can just be a private person.** If you don't ever like to leave your house, if you just like to hang out at home all the time, not be real visible and enjoy your privacy, you can do that — because you're working with an automated system and have clients all over the country, and even possibly outside of the country, and you're working out of a spare bedroom. But really, you don't even *need* a spare bedroom. You could have a computer so you could log onto your Prospect Manager. But even *that* isn't absolutely necessary. **So the business requires very little space, and it can be done in the privacy of your home.** No one has to bother you, and you don't have to bother anybody.

Number SIX: Most opportunities don't let you make money fast enough.

As I've mentioned before, the U. S. Department of Commerce says it takes 2-5 years before the average business starts to actually make a profit. With the high sale price of a lot of franchises and other business opportunities, it may take even longer for you to ever make a profit. I've mentioned that a good friend of mine has a pest control business, and it's doing about a million a year. It cost her about $600,000 to buy that company. She's had it about eight years now, and has yet to make a real profit.

Most businesses just don't make enough money fast enough! And what happens is, the people running them burn out after a while. You just see it in their eyes. You see it in their faces. One of my favorite songs is by Jackson Brown, and it's got this line in it: "He started out so young and strong, only to surrender." I see so many businesspeople where the line from that song just comes into my head. As I see it, the dream is dead. **They're working too hard for too little money,** they've given up too much of their lives, and the business just doesn't crank it out fast enough.

I've heard that a McDonald's franchise can cost as much as a million dollars. Man, how many burgers and fries do you have to sell to pay back that franchise fee? And of course, at McDonald's you've got to pay employees and overhead costs, so it's not like every 99-cent burger they sell is 100% profit toward that debt. I imagine they make a very small percentage of that dollar that they sell off their Dollar Menu. Probably a very small percentage of that actually goes to cut into their debt. And a lot of franchises — even the ones that don't cost a million dollars — require you to buy a building, and a lot of them have annual fees. You have to pay a license to use their name and all their colors, logos, and uniforms, all of that. Their fees eat you up!

Well, with CLUB-20 you can get started as an entry-level distributor for practically *nothing*. When people request your free book, we're giving away the entry level distributor position for free. But if someone were to just stumble on our website and want to buy an entry level distributor position, it's only $97. Now, we do encourage people to come to our Wealth Explosion Seminar, and if they do, you're still talking about getting started for less than a lot of people spend on a vacation. **It's very affordable, so people can get started and be in the profit extremely fast.** Your only cost is your cost to acquire the customer. Obviously, there are some expenses of doing business, but you can get in the profit really fast. Most opportunities just don't let you make money fast enough.

Number SEVEN: Most opportunities are all too much

alike, and they all try to copy each other.

I call it "marketing incest"— every company is exactly the same. **Nobody is doing anything unique.** Everybody is following the follower. It's all the same! They're taking their cues from everybody else, but it's the blind leading the blind. They don't even have a unique selling position. They all just sell the same types of products. In local businesses this is why you see, when you look in the Yellow Pages for a certain business, that all the ads look alike. How do you choose who to do business with? There's nothing to distinguish one from another. That's the kind of thing you're dealing with here. In that sense, all it takes is a little bit of differentiation, just a slightly unique selling position.

Well, one of the things that we're out to do with CLUB-20 is to help business owners transcend that boring sameness and do things to differentiate and separate themselves from everybody else. In an over-competitive, over-crowded marketplace, you've got to do something bold and audacious to stand out. **That's what we're doing here with our $60,000 in 90 days concept;** it's our message of fast cash, a promise for quick money — and showing people how that promise can actually be true. **It's something we do to separate ourselves from all of the other opportunities out there.** It also means we do unique things with all of our follow-up marketing — the way that we stay after these customers, the way we stay after these leads. I've already spoken about the way our salespeople follow-up. They stay in touch with people. These are things that nobody else is doing! **In our marketplace, there is nobody else doing things like we are.** I don't mean that in an arrogant way. They could, and they should, do these things. And yet they're not, and we are. Eventually they *will* start copying us.

Ray Kroc of McDonald's fame is one of my heroes. Back in the late 1960s, when the fast food boom was on and there were all kinds of new competitors springing up every month, somebody interviewed Ray and asked, "Ray, what about all these competitors of yours? They're copying the McDonalds system." And Ray just said, "We will innovate faster than they will copy." I love that! That's what we plan to do. They say that imitation is the sincerest form of flattery. We're proud about the fact that we have competitors who have been copying us. We'll put out something one quarter. and then we'll see that someone else will do the same thing two months later. That's fine. **We're out to be innovative. We're out to be competitive. We enjoy that whole process.** Now, I'll admit that it saddens me in a way. To me, innovation is a part of what competition is supposed to be about. And yet, it seems like there's just a lot of people who want everything to be easy and simple. They've given up, it seems. They don't put as much into it as they should. It's easier to copy what everybody else is doing, and as a result, there's not enough innovation.

And Number EIGHT: At the end of the day, when you add it all up, you'll see that most business opportunities are just loaded with pain, problems, and frustration.

People get started with the highest of hopes. They have lots of dreams, and then they just run into a lot of problems. Business isn't what it's cracked up to be. One of the reasons why we've titled this book "How to Turn Your Kitchen Table or Spare Bedroom Into a Cash Machine" is because what people really want is not a business. **What people really want is a cash machine — a money machine.** That's what we've attempted to do here. **We take care of the selling with our automatic system, and we go after the prospects like a bulldog.** It's a real partnership — you're providing the prospects and we're providing the rest. **The headaches and the hassles are all coming to us, not you.** You don't have to face that problem of wearing multiple hats. You don't have to stock inventory, or do the bookkeeping, or all the advertising to bring in new business all at the same time. **Our infrastructure does it all. You just advertise to get the prospects.** You can just sit back and relax, knowing that we'll take care of everything for you. **You can log into our new Prospect Manager from anywhere in the world.** If you're on vacation, you can log in and check out your leads and see what we're doing for you, see if you've earned any new commissions. **The whole process is totally transparent to you, so it completely eliminates most of the frustrations and pain associated with most businesses.**

You've seen all those drug commercials— where they list all the potential side effects — and most are worse than the symptoms they're supposed to cure. **What we've tried to do is take away all of the side effects of taking advantage of a business opportunity — the negative aspects of what it takes to be in business, — so you can have your own business.** We take them on. We've got a good team in place over at M.O.R.E., Inc., and we're proud of what we've done.

If you're reading this, I encourage you to come to Kansas. Even from L.A. or New York, it's only a couple of days drive if you hurry! If you want to take your time, it's a three-day drive. **Come and spend time with us, look at our operation, and see what we've done.** We're *proud* of what we've done. It's a real partnership. **It's a real team effort with you carrying part of it, and us carrying part of it.** We make money by helping you make money — so the more money we can help you make, the more money we make. **You get all of the benefits of being in business, without all of those negative side effects I've talked about throughout this book.** I encourage you to become better educated on all this. Please go back and look again at all 50 of the points that I cover here.

Anybody can say that they've got the perfect business opportunity... and everybody does say it, by the way. That's one

258

of the ways businesses copy each other. If you look through the opportunity magazines, if you read the Direct-Mail pieces you receive — they all claim to be the best. Well, if everybody is the best, how can anybody be the best? They can't be!

What I've tried to show you over the past few hundred pages are specific points of differentiation, **50 ways that CLUB-20 International is superior to every other business opportunity claiming to be the best.** We don't expect people to just believe what we're saying; we want people to shine light on this thing, to question it, and to really think about the kinds of issues that we've shared with you. **So call us, email us, or come to Kansas and investigate — and be prepared to join in the greatest business opportunity currently on the market.** I look forward to working with you!